AS THE S

Funny, Strange, and Serious Stories of Yiddishland's Jews

by Mordekhai Lipson

Translated and edited by

Jonathan Boyarin

and

Jonah Sampson Boyarin

Ben Yehuda Press

Teaneck, New Jersey

Published by Ben Yehuda Press
122 Ayers Court #1B
Teaneck, NJ 07666
http://www.BenYehudaPress.com

To subscribe to our monthly book club and support independent Jewish publishing, visit https://www.patreon.com/BenYehudaPress

Ben Yehuda Press books may be purchased at a discount by synagogues, book clubs, and other institutions buying in bulk.
For information, please email markets@BenYehudaPress.com

Cover illustration by Saul Raskin, originally for *Gut Shabbos, Gut Yor* by Zvee Hirsh Rubinstein (1937).

Text set 11.5/15 in Minion 3 by Robert Slimbach and Artifex Hand CF by Connary Fagen.

ISBN13 978-1-953829-48-1 pb

Library of Congress Cataloging-in-Publication Data

25 26 27 / 10 9 8 7 6 5 4 3 2 1   20250804

To the elders z"l of Rabbi Singer's shul,
who recalled and recounted to us,
with slivovitz and potatonik.

Contents

Translators' Introduction
In Two Hands

Jonathan writes:

Di velt dertseylt (literally, *The World Relates*), which we present here in edited translation under the title *As the Story Goes*, is a two-volume collection of anecdotes, mostly but not all about 18th- and 19th-century East European figures, mostly but not all rabbis, and virtually all men. The stories often portray these figures as praiseworthy, sometimes even saintly, but in an intimate view as a neighbor or beloved student might relate them. The collection was gathered and edited, first in the 1928 Yiddish edition that we drew on here and later in expanded Hebrew editions, by a journalist named Mordekhai Lipson, né Jawarowski in Bialystok in 1885, who had himself been trained in the traditional yeshiva world at Radin. It was in the study house that he likely first heard some of these stories: He describes the genre as a somewhat learned male oral tradition, a folklore created by "elders, smart and worthy Jews, who [in previous generations] used to sit around [telling these tales] in their study houses and humble synagogues, or at a Shabbos table or a communal celebration" (Lipson 1928, p. 11). The material reached Lipson "in some part from books, old and new, and from articles in newspapers and magazines; but the greatest part come from people who told me these stories themselves or sent them to me in letters."

One reason we chose to translate *Di velt dertseylt* is because it manages to value the traditional Jewish world of Eastern Europe without flattening its affects into hagiography, shallow nostalgia, or (as 19th-century Jewish modernizers and their ideological descendants today see it) something primitive, backward, and contemptible. It shows a religious world that is dynamic, vibrant, and self-consciously responding to contemporary economic, social, and political conditions. But first and foremost, we translated these stories because we like them, and we hope you will too. They're pithy and refined; alternately wise, ironic, or funny; and always deeply human.

The book was published at a time of cultural crisis (that is to say, in the early 20th century), when much of the lore of these generations was at risk of being forgotten. Yankev Mark's *Gdoylim fun undzer tsayt*, which contains portraits of some of the figures that appear in *As the Story Goes* and was printed in the same year as *Di velt dertseylt*, comments explicitly on the perceived massive break from the previous generation. That break was certainly exacerbated by the destruction of World War I, the repression of traditional authority under the Soviets, and the end of mass migration to the United States in the early 1920s, all of which seemed to accelerate the already rapid pace of change and dislocation that threatened the continued oral transmission of these stories. Thus, while his own introduction to the collection makes clear that it was intended as a written record of vignettes that were still circulating early in the 20th century, Lipson already sensed that they might be threatened with oblivion. We might therefore reasonably call his work salvage folklore.

In his 1928 introduction, Lipson explains that most research in Jewish folklore up to that point had focused on music and proverbs rather than oral history and biography:

> Completely set aside [from musical and proverbial folklore], bypassed and neglected, has remained the body of Jewish folklore containing stories, sayings,

habits, and character traits of Jewish luminaries and celebrities across the generations, as attested to by our people. Jews didn't write biographies of their famous figures. No, Jews don't think very much of written histories, whether of an individual or of a society. But as a result, Jews have always spoken to each other about their luminaries and notables, recounting over and over their deeds, habits, and sayings. And so it passed from tongue to tongue, from generation to generation. Thousands of such stories and sayings circulate among our people to this day. They illustrate the subjects' characters, personalities, and relationships better than any book does. That Reb Yoynesn Prager (Eibeschutz) was shrewd in worldly matters, clever enough to change the minds of ministers and kings—that we would never know from his book *Kreysi Ufleysi* nor even from his *Yaroys Dvash*. Only the stories that circulate orally among our people tell us about the kind of person he was. That Reb Akiva Eiger was a saintly man—deeply humble, deflecting even the faintest hint of praise, generously charitable, and a devoted community activist—we know not from his rabbinic responsa or from his *Gilyon Hashas*, but rather from the stories that we still tell of him today. And that Reb Ayzl Slonimer was not only incisive in his scholarship but also sharp-tongued in his everyday interactions, someone who enjoyed telling a Jewish joke and could cut someone to the quick with just a few words—this we know from the oral tradition, not from his books.

Our folk stories and sayings are a storehouse of national creativity, communicated not by formal biographers but by everyday people, reflecting the people's sentiment toward their own famous figures.

They treat each figure according to what he honestly earned through his words and deeds, and they are not compelled by decorum or piety to conceal even the flaws of any great luminary. This cultural treasure has unfortunately been neglected even by those who devote themselves to Jewish stories and folklore.

The only such tales that folklorists do not overlook are those about Hasidic saints, rebbes, and miracle workers, evoking the magical, the strange, and the mystical, which they tell and retell, print and reprint. This fascination with Hasidism stubbornly persists in our literature, especially in Yiddish. But the sayings, habits, and traits of the so-called "earthly" geniuses, luminaries, rabbis, or simply good Jews, who were neither magical nor supernatural, but instead were full of a particularly Jewish kind of decency, characterized by both compassion and common sense, whether through humble simplicity or biting insights, approaching others with a clarity of soul, with unlimited goodness and mercy—almost nobody considers these figures at all.

And worst of all is the pain of seeing the folk transmission of these stories interrupted. The elders, the good and wise Jews, who used to sit in the study houses; in the humble synagogues; at a Shabbos table; or at a celebration, and recount tales to each other of Reb Yoynesn Prager, or Reb Heshele, of the Vilna Gaon, of the *Shages Aryeh*, of Reb Chaim Volozhiner, and repeat their witty sayings— those elders are no more. Their grandchildren and great-grandchildren tell other stories about other great figures. Only here and there can you still find scattered individuals, most of them elderly men,

who remember the stories their grandfathers and
fathers had passed on to them. Some of them even
personally knew the luminaries of their generation
and are today the few who can recall and recount
their stories. And if this dwindling folk treasure is
not rescued in time, collected and recorded, then
these remnants will be lost as well, just as we have
already lost entire chapters of Jewish folklore. (Lipson 1928, v. 1, pp. 8-9)

The stories contained herein tell us more faithfully, perhaps, about
the people who told them and the man who edited them than about
the figures who feature in their narratives. As Lipson readily ac-
knowledges, we cannot take them for simple historical truth:

To be sure, this kind of approach does not address
the question of historical accuracy. We can never
be certain whether a particular great man said or
did what was related of him. Moreover, a number
of things are retold in several versions. Every region
tells the story according to its own sensibility and
appends it to someone whom they know as famous.
Thus, for example, in Lithuania the story about the
child on Kol Nidre night is attributed to Reb Yisroel
Salanter; to Reb Levi Yitschok Berdichever in Vol-
hynia; and in Galicia to Reb Moyshe Leyb Sasover.
The fine, compassionate moral is exactly the same
from each story: that we should emulate these great
rabbis, to whom a crying child is more important
than the holiest service of the year. (Lipson 1928,
v. 1, pp. 10-11)

Accordingly, a historian's thorough assessment of which stories
certainly could be or certainly couldn't be factually true is beyond
the scope of our skills and our translation project.

We come to this book almost a century after its publication. Even among those who deeply treasure and still remember large parts of the legacy and elite personalities of traditional Ashkenazi culture and learning, for the most part only those figures who wrote significant religious texts are known today, and—as was the case when Lipson wrote his introduction in 1928—primarily through the prism of their writing. One of the beauties of this collection is that it restores to us some of the "oral Torah" of those prominent authors as well as others who may have been equally well-known, valued, feared, and loved in their time but are less well-known today only because they did not leave a legacy in writing.

Lipson's collection doesn't rigidly distinguish between secular and religious, and it does not cater to a religious audience by censoring objectionable material. In this world, rabbinic authorities deal sensitively with the social and economic minutiae of their overwhelmingly impoverished communities, outfox antisemites, and intercede with government officials. Heretics, apostates, and popular writers are all learned in Talmud and *halakhah* (Jewish law) and use its rhetoric to fashion their critiques of religious tradition. The stories thus appeal to a shared sense of Jewishness that does not distinguish neatly between religion, culture, and morality.

Unlike much traditional religious Jewish scholarship dealing with topics such as individual morality, correct daily practice, or Talmudic commentary, Lipson's Yiddish volumes include no letters of approval from rabbinic figures, suggesting approval may not have been necessary to his audience (or alternatively, may have been impossible to obtain). Nevertheless, the collection as a whole resists any notion that religious or traditional figures were losing authority because they were hidebound, repressive, or unimaginative. Our selections from this Yiddish treasure tend to emphasize that resistance. Thus, a number of the stories emphasize the halakhic flexibility of rabbinic authorities in contrast to more modern rabbis, or in the face of poverty. In one of the longer stories, for example, a Reform rabbi is heard insisting that—despite his more liberal commitments—he nevertheless always rules strictly in matters of *kashrus* (kosher laws) because he doesn't wish to be seen as overly lenient. The parable within the story mocks such inflexibility, and suggests that the traditional Reb Chaim Rappoport, in contrast, has the confidence that comes from close familiarity with a nuanced, polyphonic tradition and allows him a more dynamic response, including providing a lenient ruling under certain circumstances (story 52).* An example of flexibility in the face of poverty is a vignette about Reb Shayele Kutner, who played on the literal and metaphorical meanings of bitterness in order to permit a poor woman to eat a chicken (story 169). This flexibility, we contend, reflects a resilience and openness to cultural and material contingency which is part of the living tradition.

Any conception of Torah and halakhic tradition as dynamic and potentially compassionate faces twin challenges today. On the one hand, Western Christianity and secularism tend to cast Jewish tradition as hopelessly hidebound, unfeeling, and always-being-superseded, something to be nostalgically visited through the occasional Yiddish expression, tchotchkes, or viewings of *Fiddler on the Roof* at best, or to simply be forgotten. And on the other hand, traditionalist Orthodox Jews—the only ones remaining who tell stories of the figures featured in *Di velt dertseylt*—tend to portray themselves as the natural inheritors of a seamless (and thus static) line of cultural practices. The traditionalist Orthodox Jewish world's development of ever stricter practices around kashrus, appearance, and gender roles, intended to defend communal integrity, tends to be accompanied by the implicit assumption that these practices are how it always was. The community's increasing stringency and reliance on a narrative of stringency as traditional have left diminished room for stories in which revered historical rabbis rule leniently.

There are about 1,000 anecdotes in the Yiddish version of Lipson's collection, not all of which are readily translatable. Many of

---

* We have retained the numbers identifying each story in the Yiddish original, both for the convenience of those who might want to consult that text and to underscore how much more there is than we present in this volume and in the voices, ears, and memory of the people.

those we included were simply personal favorites, the kind of story where a protagonist delighted us with surprising resourcefulness or generosity. But not all of the stories in the book—and not all we translated—fit that bill. We included a few stories we don't like so much, ones that come off as mean, such as one about a traveling cantor who tricks an innkeeper into giving him shelter for the night by promising riches he can't deliver (story 209). Some contain a parable that gives a richly atmospheric and evocative sense of shtetl life, even if the moral of the story doesn't work perfectly.

Some stories are famous from other sources, such as Reb Mendele Kotsker's sharp rebuke to an arrogant young scholar (story 233) or Reb Levi Yitschok's defense of simple working people (story 254). Some have well-known variants elsewhere, told along the same lines but with a different narrative arc and a similar moral, such as the tale of Reb Zushe and Reb Elimelech's rebuke to someone who only offered them hospitality when he realized they were great men (story 288). Some are told elsewhere with different protagonists, such as the story of Reb Ayzl Kharif answering a question about why a rich man will more readily give to a poor cripple than to a poor scholar, which is also told in the name of the Dubner Maggid (story 927). A story about prudent investment and love of the Land of Israel, told here in the name of Reb Shayele Kutner, is elsewhere told in the name of Moses Mendelssohn (story 14).

Not all of the stories depend on specifics of Jewish culture and language, and differences in Jewish culture are also represented. In one story, Reb Zundl Salanter reminds a coachman that all of his acts are seen from above (story 291). In another, Reb Naftoli Ropshitser sees through the guise of someone who comes to confess his sins (story 312). Indeed, one could imagine this latter story easily being told—*lehavdil* (to preserve the distinction)—of a Catholic country priest. And at least one story expresses hesitance about the movement to settle the Land of Israel (story 356), but early Zionists are represented here as well.

Several themes are represented in these stories. As a father and son team ourselves, the affection and tensions between scholarly fathers and sons was one theme we were drawn to. One such story finds Reb Chaim, the founder of the Volozhin Yeshiva, quick to take offense and his son, Reb Itsele, equally quick to reassure his father of his own filial respect (story 216). Another story has the young Reb Chaim Soloveichik defending his own scholarly insight in the face of his father Reb Yoshe Ber's withering dismissal (story 239). Another theme represented in these stories is the management of rabbinic rivalries. As you read story 239, pay close attention to who's who, because the story manages to flummox the reader almost as much as its protagonist does the waiting townspeople. There are stories about a great man who can't find the person he needs to forgive (story 380), or about a great man traveling incognito and quietly bearing insult and injury (story 398). Several stories are about figures who aid others at the expense of their own spouses and families (stories 392, 393, 429). Some of these stories even give us clues to why orally retold folktales about historical figures such as these may be exaggerated or entirely invented, such as the one in which Reb Chaim Brisker (Soloveichik) rebukes newspaper journalists for putting words in his mouth (story 465).

As Lipson notes, several of these stories are in the genre known to the West as the Hasidic tale (though they include little of the supernatural). This relies on a double stereotype: that Hasidic masters were uniquely poetic and sensitive, and that Lithuanian/Misnagdic masters, designated here quite literally by their opposition to Hasidism, were uniquely scholarly and rationalist. Lipson himself was from the Lithuanian/Misnagdic sphere; his Yiddish and the bulk of the selections in his book reflect that. Nevertheless, this collection suggests that the division between the two camps was hardly as neat as commonly perceived. Many Hasidic masters were deeply learned and intolerant of fools, and Lithuanian masters were often famous for their acts of great humility, restraint, and kindness.

As mentioned above, Lipson knew that—tied though they are to people who lived and died in the real world—these stories are not "history." He included, for example, two conflicting accounts of how Reb Meshulem Igra became the rabbi of Pressburg (stories

685 and 694). In one anecdote, Moyshe Rozenson is described as a missionary (story 682), and in another only as suspected of missionizing (story 689). On the other hand, at least a few of the stories here—such as the one about the Jew forced to convert before Passover—are relatively well known but usually in stripped-down versions lacking the rich milieu and attribution to historical figures that Lipson provides (story 515).

To the extent that these stories seem to present behavioral exemplars for us, they do not all present the same models. One describes Reb Oyzer of Klementov, author of the *Even Oyzer*, as someone who could get by as long as he had a goat to milk (story 102). And yet, there's also a story here in which the Rizhiner Rebbe justifies his material attachments and rejects asceticism (story 302). Thus, this project (and the folk culture behind it) is not attempting to be completely systematic. We're not all supposed to be like the Even Oyzer and the Rizhiner. We can't be, because they have opposing tendencies. It's easy to see a resonance with the way that the Talmud shows many different types of rabbinic heroes: humble and proud, active in the world and secluded in the study house, lenient and strict, and occasionally flawed. This resonance does not strike us as incidental. The figures featured in these stories, as well as the people who recounted them, were deeply learned in the Talmud. That polyphonic tradition provided them with ample models for how to conduct themselves as well as how to shape stories.

A few of the stories here even seem similar in form and message to stories from the Talmud. The one about Reb Pinches's technique for avoiding arrogance upon taking up his new rabbinical post (story 104) recalls the great scholar Rava's trick for not getting a swelled head when crowds followed him (BT Yoma 87a). Another shows Reb Yankev Lissa reassuring a colleague after the latter had been shown greater honor in the synagogue (story 341). In late antique Babylonia, too, rabbis were concerned about their relative prestige while attempting to remain humble:

Rabbi Abbahu and Rabbi Ḥiyya bar Abba happened to come to a certain place. Rabbi Abbahu taught matters of *aggada*, and at the same time Rabbi Ḥiyya bar Abba taught *halakhah*. Everyone left Rabbi Ḥiyya bar Abba and went to Rabbi Abbahu, and Rabbi Ḥiyya was offended.

Rabbi Abbahu said to him, to appease him: "I will tell you a parable: To what is this matter comparable? It is comparable to two people, one who sells precious stones and one who sells small items. To whom do the customers rush? Don't they rush to the one who sells small items? Similarly, you teach lofty and important matters that do not attract many people. Everyone comes to me because I teach minor matters." (BT Sotah 40a, adapted from Sefaria translation)

Certainly Reb Pinches knew the story about Rava, and Reb Yankev of Lissa knew the one about Rabbi Abahu and Rabbi Ḥiyya bar Abba. Now you also know the ones about Reb Pinches and Reb Yankev.

Creating *As the Story Goes* has been a slow process, especially in our attempts to preserve the rich range of cultural allusions that give these stories their power while making them at least potentially accessible to an audience that, at minimum, does not know Yiddish.

What will be the future of this particular transmission?

What do we really mean when we repeat the dictum that the lips of the Sages move in the grave when their sayings are repeated in their name? (BT Sanhedrin 90b)

What links are created between the authors of these anecdotes, their original recorders or storytellers, Lipson, the Boyarins, and those future readers?

How will these stories circulate in their new clothes?

Who will tell these stories next, and in what tongues?

Jonah writes:

As my father notes, Mordekhai Lipson collected these stories during the interwar period, in the face of accelerating pressures to assimilate and forget. A century later, one can't help but read them with the awareness of the even more violent and rapid breaches in transmission that would soon follow, caused by the Holocaust and mass immigrations of global Jewry to Palestine and Israel. I have the dizzying sense that this world is utterly foreign yet utterly mine. So any chance of making something useful of my veil of alienation and misunderstanding—and of the deep, if humanly flawed, cultural resources that await me on the other side—lies in the work of sustained, honest encounter with the sources of both my alienation and my attachment. I started this translation project because my father said I might like to read these stories, and he was right. I read them with pleasure, and often rapt attention. Each story transmitted from Lipson to me felt like an act of recovery, for the tradition and for myself. A decade ago, I would not have been able to translate them.

But to fight oblivion is not necessarily to recall everything. The stories of women, disabled people, queer people, and others on the margins of society go almost entirely overlooked in this volume. We see no female protagonists; the few women described here tend to serve as foils to demonstrate a rabbi's total absorption in the spiritual world (story 498), willingness to breach the strict letter of the law in order to aid the poor and suffering (story 169), or punctilious impartiality and incorruptibility (story 118). Lipson tells us that the stories were recounted by learned men, in the patriarchal and (at that time) exclusively homosocial world of the beis medresh, the study house. We do not know Lipson's tendencies as a collector and editor in this regard, other than to note what he published. Stories in this genre featuring female protagonists may well have circulated in this world even if they are omitted in Lipson's collection. To this day, Belzer Hasidim print Yiddish tales of their rebbetsin from two centuries past, of how she shaped her husband the first Belzer Rebbe's career, and how she instructed his Hasidim to be more pious with respect to everyday domestic matters (see *Pininey Koydesh*, 5782, Parshas R'ey).

Lipson included a few stories whose "punchline" is gender hierarchy and separation. We did not include them in the body of our translation because we primarily selected those stories which we enjoyed and hope others will enjoy. Pleasure in the received tradition is, I think, a virtue, one that encourages both greater learning and action. But so, too, is honesty, a value Lipson claims for these stories when he describes them (as my father relates above) as "reflecting the people's sentiment toward their own famous figures... not compelled by decorum or piety to conceal even the flaws of this or that great luminary." In that spirit, here is one example of the sort of traditional and explicit sexism that Lipson included in *As the Story Goes*.

> A new synagogue was built in Memel. Some extra bricks were left over from the construction. Reb Yisroel Salanter was asked what should be done with the remaining bricks, since they had obviously been intended for a sacred use.
>
> "The most sensible approach would be," Reb Yisroel answered, "to wall up the entrance to the women's balcony. It would be better if the women sat at home and watched the children." (story 168)

I am sorry to be the messenger of these blithely cruel words, of which I was ignorant in the fall of 2017, when I published an article in *Jewish Currents* under the title, "Men: Cook, Clean and Do the Childcare This Yom Kippur," built around a different Reb Yisroel Salanter story from Lipson's collection. I interpreted that one as a traditional model for contemporary Jewish feminist men. It goes like this:

> One Yom Kippur, Reb Yisroel Salanter was late to Kol Nidrei. Naturally, the entire congregation

waited for him: You couldn't start until he had said Kol Nidrei. They waited and waited—it grew quite late—but Reb Yisroel still wasn't there. So the shammes was sent over to his house: No one was home! They had all gone to hear Kol Nidrei.

The congregation began to grow agitated, worrying that, God forbid, something had happened to Reb Yisroel. So they set off in search of him. They looked and asked around, but he was nowhere to be found, so they started to make their way back to the synagogue. One of them happened to glance through the window of a nearby home, and he was shocked and amazed to see Reb Yisroel sitting by a cradle and gently rocking the child inside it.

They ran into the home, crying: "Rabbi! Don't you know, we've been looking everywhere for you. We're waiting for you before we start Kol Nidrei."

"Shhh," Reb Yisroel replied, "You'll wake the babe. It only just fell asleep. When shul, I heard a child's cry. So I went into this room and no one was here. They had all gone to synagogue. So I sat down to rock the babe, until it had fallen asleep..." (story 564)

Having now read both Reb Yisroel stories together, I see a figure who at one moment enacts a surprising and saintly anti-patriarchal reversal by valorizing one child's care over his entire community's davening, and at another moment blithely and callously reinforces the gendered separation of the worlds of male-davening and female-childcare. Or more generously, one might say that the throughline between the two stories is that Reb Yisroel thinks that childcare is more important than going to shul—for everyone, including himself.

I am trying to explain here how I read these stories, both as a suggestion for how you might read them and also as a window into my motivations as a translator. I try not to think of our modern world (whatever that may mean, when the world is so terribly fractured, and when Jewish communities are so stupendously various) as being in some simple way better or more advanced than the world that breathes through the pages of *As the Story Goes*. Likewise, I try not to view our present life as intrinsically less holy or virtuous than that of the Jews who told these tales of Reb Yisroel. But we certainly have our differences, and they are instructive.

I grew up in the 1990s and early 2000s among poor, elderly Jewish immigrants in the Lower East Side, particularly spending time with them in shul on Shabbos. They seem so terribly far away now that it is difficult to discern what their world has to do with ours. I rarely hear their mother tongue, Yiddish, spoken in full conversation in the non-Hasidic shuls I go to, or among non-Hasidic Ashkenazi Jews in almost any setting, for that matter. My childhood elders' realistic assessment of the world as an ever-growing pile of ruins among which we stubbornly cling to one another and enact Yiddishkeit—lightly, wryly, grouchily, unpretentiously, insouciantly, insistently, and (on occasion) reverently—and their conception of Jewish community as being as much a source of bread for the hungry as it is of Torah for the learned have been supplanted in many middle- and upper-class Jewish communities by a stiffness, a white Protestant-inflected conception of synagogue as the site for prayer and ethics. (This is in part the direct result of an ideological effort initiated by wealthy assimilationist German American Jews in the early 20th century, as attested to in Allen Lipson's 2022 essay, "The Sanitizing of Conservative Judaism.") Although I can no longer hear the voices of those elders of blessed memory when I go to shul, I feel their echoes in the gestalt of *As the Story Goes*, and I am haunted by the conviction that we need their world, which we have so carelessly abandoned. I am convinced, too, that these ancestors need their descendants (construed as broadly as you'd like) to inherit their world: not to replicate it, but to learn from it, and to make a *tikkun* (a social or cosmic repair) on the brokenness created by their patriarchy.

More: I claim that the whole world has something necessary to learn from these stories. Christian Europe has colonized, conquered, and economically, culturally, and politically dominated the globe for almost half of a millennium. Many people today, including me, are committed to overturning abusive systems of dominance, to resisting Christian white supremacy, to building a multi-racial, multi-religious, feminist society founded on widely shared prosperity. Part of this commitment is the necessary work of what Kenyan intellectual Ngugi wa Thiong'o termed as "decolonizing our minds," of unlearning patterns of subjugation, exploitation, and hatred of the marginalized self and other, and of robustly imagining alternative ways of being, informed by minority traditions and futuristic fantasies. We have a lot to learn about this project from European Jews who survived over a millennium of Christian European economic, cultural, and political violence and domination.

As the Story Goes shows us 18th-, 19th-, and 20th-century Eastern and Central European Jews generating enormous creativity in the intellectual, political, and cultural realms to respond to new forms of institutional antisemitism. As European nation-states modernized and coalesced around distinct, often monolithic, national and racial identities, they began to consider their subjects—including Jews—as citizens who must conform to their various national projects, including language, education, dress, names, and identity, or else be eliminated through pogroms, expulsion, conversion, or genocide. Some Jews acceded in part or in whole to these demands, giving up many parts of Jewish difference and/or adopting ideologies such as political Zionism that mimicked the European ethno-nationalist model. Others attempted to negotiate at times competing commitments to their Yiddishkeit and to international, cross-ethnic, cross-religious workers' movements.

But by and large these stories are not theirs. Rather, they belong to figures who cast themselves as protecting both Jews and Yiddishkeit through traditional means. Many of them rejected Zionism, Communism, and Bundism on religious terms, although a few of the figures are implicitly or explicitly sympathetic to one or another of these movements. Instead, they resisted antisemitism and assimilationism by means of the ingenious political intercession of select communal representatives (such as in stories 29-43) as well as through a sustained refusal to internalize the Christian European denigration of Jews as inherently inferior and superseded (such as in stories 6, 48, or 598). This is not to say that theirs was the "right" model. First of all, I don't think any such thing even exists: in every time and place, we must receive (or recover) whatever pieces of wisdom we can from our ancestors and neighbors, while humbly but not timidly making meaning of them for our own time and place. To demand our ancestors be the perfect model for us is to tell them that they may never have lived for themselves, and to abrogate our own responsibility (the same responsibility every generation has, until the Messiah comes) for making the best of our broken world. Second, the stories in which relatively powerless Jews outfox their perniciously antisemitic rulers may well have been fantasies rather than historical occurrences. But not "just" fantasies—they reflect the lively, resistant imagination and cultural memory of the beis medrash at a time of vicious subjugation.

For me, these traditionalist Jewish stories are necessary but hardly sufficient resources for how to do my part for justice, be a Jew, and serve God. The stories are focused on men; often Jewish-chauvinist; more focused on relieving individual cases of economic suffering among the Jewish poor than ending the exploitation of all working people (though we may find a few hints of rabbinic critiques of capitalism scattered across the collection, such as in in story 480); and do not remark on the Western economy's enslavement and exploitation of the global South, which some other Jewish contemporaries certainly did. Learning a Reb Yisroel Salanter story doesn't mean we can dispense, God forbid, with bell hooks or Edward Said. But I do suggest that Reb Yisroel stories might be read alongside their work, and the work of other important feminist, anti-racist, and anti-colonialist thinkers. In order to do so, I suggest—to borrow Eve Sedgwick's term from her book *Touching Feeling*—a "reparative reading" that makes whatever good use we can of the resources we have inherited for resistance and reimagination, while doing our very best not to replicate their mistakes in our own lives.

The act of collective liberation, while an awesome—perhaps even messianic—goal, is not the only thing that brings me to this project. I have inherited a distinct, although not unique, Jewish tradition of taking pleasure in the world-that-is, experiencing joy and humor among all the brokenness, a tradition which goes back to at least the times of the Babylonian Talmud. This capacity for pleasure, which I hope you will find in many of these stories, is a compass that points us toward what a liberated future might feel like and provides us with energy to fight for it in the present. I hope you can share in the profound affection and amusement that these Jewish stories evince when they tease revered rabbis as well as collective Jewry.

Because pleasure is within the political, our choice to more-or-less include those stories which we liked best is in part a political one. I confess that some of these editorial and translation choices on my part are meant to be persuasive—to persuade you that this world you are about to enter is dynamic, lovable, and worth re-membering. It has felt like an impossible task at times, imagining myself as another link in the chain that carried these stories from an 18th-century study house to Mordekhai Lipson, from Lipson to me and my father, from us to you. It overwhelms me at times, my attempt to continue this chain in the face of the rupture in trans-mission of Yiddish language, religious tradition, and Ashkenazi cultural memory that occurred across the violent paroxysms and overwhelming assimilatory pressures that transformed Jewish life in the 20th century. And so I have risked over-compensating: My translations often lean toward making the stories smoother, more comprehensible to a wider audience, sometimes at the cost of the particularity of the stories' language or the world they depict. My father leans towards a more faithful style of translation, sometimes at the cost of clarity or accessibility.

I hope that our process—which ultimately settled on him fashion-ing the first draft, me taking the second, and us working on them from there—combines the best of each of our translation tendencies.

But we have certainly performed in many places the necessary failures of the translator to transport an entire world. So what you have before you are lovely fragments, a hodgepodge of treasures rescued from a ravaged world, or, as bell hooks put it, "memories like reused fabric in a crazy quilt" (I first read these words in the form of the epigraph to my father's 1992 work, *Storm from Paradise).* They are equally reflective of the many hands that have worked them over the centuries as of the cultures that once birthed them. Now they lie in your hands as well. They belong to us now, imperfect heirs that we may be. They are for us to learn and make our own sense of. So don't feel like you need to get everything just right in order to say to your friends, "Well you know, as the story goes..."

*   *   *

We are extremely grateful to the Yiddish Book Center for a 2020-21 translation fellowship that helped us shape our own sense of how to approach these texts, and to Rose Waldman, a judicious and knowledgeable mentor. Thanks as well to both Daniel Boyarin and Elli Stern for consultation on certain points of translation and history. Thank you to Jacqueline (Nekhe) Krass for hitting some metaphorical late free-throws in the clutch with her careful copy-editing, and to Elizabeth Shulman-Nadolny for finding the Saul Raskin illustration for the cover. Finally, thank you to Ben Yehuda Press and their thorough editing team, especially Laura Logan and Dainy Bernstein.

*   *   *

A word about transliteration: We have attempted to follow common orthography where there is a conventional spelling in English (thus, "Chaim" rather than "Khayem," or "Mendelssohn" rather than "Mendelson.") Otherwise, our default has been to use the standard YIVO system, in which "ay" is pronounced like the "i" in "wine"; "ey" like the "ey" in convey; "a" like the "a's" in "llama"; and "o" like a shorter version of the "aw" in "awesome," etc. Our goal throughout has been readability and ease of further research.

*   *   *

We have organized the stories we selected into sections using Lipson's own thematic headings. We have treated both volumes of *As the Story Goes* as a single volume, so you will sometimes see story numbers that appear out of order, as a given thematic section includes stories from both volumes. Volume One of the Yiddish ends with story 590, and Volume Two begins with 591. So, for instance, in this text the opening section, "The Jewish People," jumps from story 88 to 592, as it is the opening section to both volumes.

As the Story Goes

ריינקל, לייפניקער רב, איז א מאל

ז ער האט יענעם און יענעם בא׳גנב

אט האט ער עם מיט זיך, זאל עם

מורא געהט פאר א בלבול. זאגט ע

שט צום גלח.

בי, — חידוש׳ט זיך דער גנב — איר ש

טו מיד — ענטפערט אים ר׳ ברוך —

וואס מ׳איז זיך פאר אים מתוודו

※

ייזלש, וואַרשעווער רב, איז אמאל גע

ים אין וואַגאַן איז געזעסן א רוסיש

מיט א כלב. האט ער גערופן דעם כלב

נעבאך, אויפן הונט — רופט זיך אפ ה

ו נאמען.

פרעגט דער פאלקאוווניק.

גט ר׳ בעריש — וואלט ער געווען א

כלל ישראל

The Jewish People

5

A thief once came to Reb Boruch Frankel, the rabbi of Leipzig, and confessed that he had robbed a certain person. But now he wanted to return the stolen item. He had it with him and was eager to hand it over to the rabbi.

Reb Boruch was afraid of getting mixed up in a scandal. So he said to the thief, "Take it to the Catholic priest instead."

"What are you talking about, Rabbi? You're sending a Jew to a *priest*?"

"Naturally," answered Reb Boruch. "Anything told in confession a priest is forbidden to reveal."

6

Reb Berish Meisels, the rabbi of Warsaw, was once riding the train. Across from him happened to be sitting a Russian colonel, a terrible antisemite, who had a dog that he kept calling by a Jewish name, "Yankl."

Reb Berish spoke up. "That poor dog, it's a pity it has a Jewish name."

"Oh yeah? Why?" asked the colonel.

"If not," said Reb Berish, "they'd have made him a colonel."

7

Reb Berish Halpern, the Maggid (Preacher) of Lublin, was once the victim of blood libel, and was taken to jail. He managed to keep his tallis and tefillin with him when he went in, and he would pray with them every day, very loudly, as was his custom. The warden of the prison soon grew fed up with it.

"Why," he asked, "do you have to shout like that when you pray?"

"I'm a Jew. That's how we pray," answered Reb Berish.

"Why can't you pray quietly, like we do?"

"I'll tell you, honored sir. You have your God close to you, pinned up right here on the wall, so you can pray quietly. But our God is very high up, far away in Heaven. So when we pray, we have to shout."

8

The General Governor of Warsaw once went to visit Lodz. Various officials waited to greet him at the train station, including the leaders of the three religious communities: the Russian Orthodox priest, the Polish Catholic priest, and—*lehavdil*—the Jewish rabbi. As always, the two priests stood in front, with the rabbi behind them.

After the reception, Reb Elye Chaim was approached by the mayor of Lodz, who was a good friend of his, and asked, "Tell me the truth, Rabbi. Didn't you resent having the representatives of the other two religions in front, while you, who represent the oldest religion, stood in the back?"

"God forbid!" responded Reb Elye Chaim. "You know that my religion is the mother of those two religions, and a mother never resents her own children."

12

In Dvinsk, in the Russian Empire, there once lived a scribe of religious articles named Reb Yitschok Note. He was an upright and God-fearing man, like Jewish scribes used to be. He had two unmarried sons, each as God-fearing as himself.

One of the sons was summoned by the draft committee and forcibly conscripted. It happened to be a good year overall, with many Jews released from service, but Reb Yitschok Note's son was not so fortunate.

Some young wise guys mocked the scribe: "What have you got to say now, Reb Yitschok Note? You see? They released the boys who aren't religious, and your pious son they drafted."

"It's like this," answered Reb Yitschok Note. "The Tsar has ordered both Jews and Gentiles to be drafted. So they take real Gentiles and real Jews. Thank God, my son is a real Jew, so he was drafted. But those lowlifes who are neither Jews nor Gentiles were released."

14

As is well known, Reb Shayele Kutner was one of the first proponents of the Chovevei Tzion (Lovers of Zion) movement and was deeply committed to a Jewish homeland in Israel.

A Jewish merchant once came to him seeking advice about a plan to do business there.

"So do you plan, then," asked Reb Shayele, "to travel to the Land of Israel?"

"No, Rebbe. I'm staying here, but I want to send money and have someone arrange deals for me over there."

Reb Shayele understood that if this man tried to do business in Israel without actually being there, the odds were good he'd lose his entire investment, and then he might complain about Jewish settlement in the Land of Israel. So he smiled and replied, "I've seen Jews who leave their money behind in the diaspora and travel to the Land of Israel to be buried there. But I've never seen a Jew remain in the diaspora and send his money to be buried in the Land of Israel."

15

A Jew once came to Reb Yitschok Meir, the Rebbe of Ger, to seek his advice about traveling to the Land of Israel.

Reb Yitschok Meir responded, "It's more important to travel to the Jew of your land—your Rebbe—than to the land of the Jews."

22

Reb Chaim Volozhiner once said:
"This is how Moshiach will arrive.
"I'll be sitting in my office studying, as usual. My wife will run in and shout, 'Chaim, how can you keep sitting and studying? Moshiach came!'
"I'll spit three times and say, 'Tfu! Who told you so?'
"'Go out into the marketplace,' she'll say, 'and you'll see. Not a child left in its cradle. Everyone has left to greet Moshiach...'"

23

Reb Leyb, the rebbe known as the Shpoler Zeyde, once said: "Lord, you keep the Jews in exile, waiting for them to repent. I swear to you on my beard and on my peyos, it's the other way around: The Jews will not repent until Moshiach comes."

24

In the Hebrew year 5600 (1839-1840 C.E.), Jews in Poland talked themselves into believing Moshiach was about to come. They had discovered some kind of allusions to it in the numerical values of Hebrew words. As time went by, more and more Jews grew convinced that *tof-reysh*, the Hebrew year 5600, was the year of Redemption. They were called the "*tar*-niks."
The Rabbi of Warsaw, Reb Yankev Gesundheit, was afraid that the *tar*-niks might (God forbid!) develop into a new heresy, like the followers of Shabtai Tsvi. So he got up in the synagogue and said, "I swear on this Torah scroll, this year Moshiach is definitely *not* coming."

25

Reb Meirl of Premishlan once said: "If Moshiach wants to come peacefully, then we'll eagerly await him. But if he's going to arrive with righteous fury, bringing all the birth-pangs of the World to Come—then we'll kindly excuse him. Better he not come at all."

29

The Jewish philosopher Solomon Maimon spent his final years in the household of a Prussian baron, at an estate near Breslau. When Maimon died, the baron sent the body to Breslau so that he could be buried in a Jewish grave. Since Maimon was a famous heretic, the burial society asked the rabbi, Reb Yitschok Yoysef Teumim, what they should do with the body. The rabbi ruled that the purification rituals should not be performed, that the body should be buried next to the fence, and that all of Maimon's manuscripts should be burned. And so it was done.

When the baron found out, he reported the Jewish community to the authorities, who summoned the rabbi and asked him, "Why did the Jews give such a great scholar such a terrible insult?"

"God forbid," answered Reb Yitschok Yoysef. "No one insulted him. On the contrary, we did everything to honor him!

"We didn't do the purification ritual, because when he was alive he didn't believe in it. We didn't bury him with the other bodies, because we Jews have a custom of burying each category of person in a different row. Rabbis are buried next to each other, and pillars of the community are buried together. We didn't have a row for philosophers yet, so we started a new row with him. And we burned his manuscripts, because not one of us is worthy to read them."

28

Reb Yoynesn of Prague was well-liked by the royal house. The king appreciated his wisdom and liked to chat with him.

One time Reb Yoynesn was on his way to the study house, when the king ran into him. The king asked, "Where are you headed?"

"I don't know, Your Highness!" answered Reb Yoynesn.

This answer angered the king so much that he ordered Reb Yoynesn thrown in jail.

That evening, when the king's anger had cooled off, he ordered that Reb Yoynesn be brought before him.

The king asked, "What were you thinking, giving me an answer like that? Don't you know that mocking the king is an act of rebellion?"

"God forbid, Your Highness!" answered Reb Yoynesn. "I wasn't making fun of you. It's the simple truth: A person never knows where he's going. See—I thought I was walking to the study house, but here I ended up in jail!"

30

When Maria Theresa, the ruler of Austria, issued an order expelling the Jews from all of Bohemia, the Jews sent the rabbinical judge of Prague, Reb Zalmen Korev, to entreat one of the cabinet ministers to have the decree withdrawn.

Reb Zalmen Korev went to the minister and pleaded for the Jews of Bohemia. In his great distress, Reb Zalmen burst into loud weeping.

"But why are you making such an unseemly clamor?" asked the minister.

"Because," answered Reb Zalmen, "it's not just me who's weeping. Thousands of other Jews cry out through me."

32

Reb Itsele Volozhiner presided over the first rabbinical assembly in St. Petersburg, during the reign of Nicholas the First. Since he was the leading rabbinical authority of his generation, the government paid him special attention. Uvarov, the minister of education, wanted to convince him—and through him the rest of the rabbis—that

Jews should educate their children in secular subjects, stop wearing their long coats, cut off their peyos, and so forth. Uvarov's model was Dr. Max Lilienthal, a German rabbi who played a significant role in that period. Lilienthal traveled to various Jewish communities trying to convince people to cooperate with the authorities, dress in a more modern fashion, and send their children to the government schools.

During the assembly, Minister Uvarov asked Reb Itsele: "*Ravin*, why do you have to wear such a long undergarment with fringes so long they hang below your shirt? Can't one be a pious Jew and wear a small undergarment with short fringes near your heart? Take Dr. Lilienthal for example—he's a rabbi, a pious Jew, and he certainly wears fringes, but you don't see them."

"Let me tell you, Lord Minister," answered Reb Itsele. "We Jews wear fringes in order to remember the commandments that God gave us. As it is written: '*U-re'isem oso u-zkhartem*—and you shall see them, and you shall remember.' Now Dr. Lilienthal is an educated man with a sharp mind and a good memory. For him, a small undergarment with short fringes can suffice. But me, I'm an old-fashioned rabbi with an aging mind. My memory isn't what it once was. So in order to remember our commandments, I must wear a large undergarment with long fringes."

34

When Moses Montefiore, the British Jewish advocate and philanthropist, was visiting Vilna, Reb Yoysef Zakheim, the most prominent Jew in the city, invited Montefiore to his home. Montefiore arrived, accompanied by his secretary and various other Jewish dignitaries. Over dinner, he spoke about his journey to St. Petersburg and the conversation he'd had with a tsarist minister there.

"I asked the minister," Montefiore said, "why Jews were being driven out of the countryside. 'What are you talking about?' he said. 'Who's driving them out? Let them stay there.'"

Among those listening was Reb Yankev Volf, the rabbi of Nemetsin, who at that time was working as a private tutor for Zakheim's children. He was easily upset. When he heard how casually the minister had dismissed Montefiore's question, he realized that Montefiore's intervention had been useless. He became distraught and burst out weeping. Everyone was embarrassed at this breach of etiquette in the presence of the great Montefiore.

"Why is this man weeping?" asked Montefiore.

Reb Avrom Zakheim, Reb Yoysef's son, responded, "This man used to live in a country village, and then they expelled him."

39

When Reb Nochemke was the rabbi of Grodno, the governor was a bitter antisemite, a real Haman. He subjected the Jews of his province to untold misery. But he possessed a very high opinion of Reb Nochemke. He knew Reb Nochemke to be an upright and honest man—a saint.

On Novy God the leaders of the Jewish community, with Reb Nochemke at their head, paid a visit to the governor to offer their best wishes for the new year. As was customary, the governor received them, and in the usual fashion they wished him "a new year with new fortune."

Once they had conveyed these formal wishes, the governor indicated that they could go. He asked Reb Nochemke to stay behind.

When everyone else had gone, the governor turned to Reb Nochemke and said, "Don't think they're fooling me. I know that the Jews despise me. They're not my friends—I'm too hard on them. When you gave me those New Year wishes, you were just doing it because you had to, because you fear me. In your hearts you wished me something quite different, I'm sure.

"Coming from the others, it's no surprise—they're ordinary people. But I am very surprised at you, Reb Nochemke. An upright, honest person, a man who always speaks the truth—how can you say one thing while thinking the opposite?"

"God forbid," replied Reb Nochemke. "We all sincerely meant what we said. We wished you a new year with new fortune. What does 'new fortune' mean for someone like you? It means you should be promoted to a higher rank, to General Governor—or even a cabinet minister!

"If that happened, you would leave Grodno. And that is something the Jews of Grodno wish for with all our hearts."

43

The Austrian emperor, Franz Josef II, was a kindly ruler and fond of Jews. Whenever he came to Krakow, he was in the habit of visiting the main Jewish synagogue as well as the Christian church. The emperor's portrait always hung in the anteroom of the synagogue.

It turned out once, shortly before the emperor was set to arrive and everyone had assembled to greet him, that the portrait had somehow disappeared. By the time someone noticed this, it was too late—the emperor had already arrived! He saw that his portrait was missing and asked the rabbi, Reb Shimen Sofer, for an explanation.

"I'm very happy to explain, Your Highness," answered Reb Shimen. "We Jews are obligated to put on tefillin each day. For us they are a symbol, a sign of our Jewishness. But when we are visited by the holy Sabbath, we do not wear tefillin, and indeed we're not even allowed to touch them, because the Sabbath itself is so great and holy that we are forbidden to have anything to do with lesser symbols.

"It's the same thing with your portrait, Your Highness. When you aren't with us, we have your portrait to remind us of you. But when we have the honor of seeing you in person, we must not display your portrait, which is merely a likeness of you—so much less than your great presence."

48

During the unrest in Vilna, more than forty Jewish young adults were arrested on suspicion of belonging to the Nihilists. The next morning, the General Governor of Vilna summoned the Jewish leaders of Vilna. And they came: Reb Matisyahu Strashun, Reb Yankele Kovner, Reb Shmuel Peskin and Reb Zalmen Reb Uri's. The

General Governor strode in and angrily spat out, "So, in addition to all of your other virtues, you Jews had to become Nihilists as well?"

When they heard this, the Jewish leaders were terrified. The first one to recover his voice was Reb Yankele Kovner. He asked, "*We are Nihilists?*"

"It's your children!" insisted the General Governor. "That's how you teach them!"

"Please don't be offended, Governor," responded Reb Yankele. "But as long as we were teaching our own children, in our cheders and yeshivas, there were no nihilists among us. As soon as you started teaching our children in your schools, this is how they've been turning out."

52

Reb Chaim Rappoport once had an encounter with a German Reform rabbi. The latter wasn't a great Torah scholar, but as might be expected, he was well-versed in secular knowledge. So the Reform rabbi acted arrogantly toward Reb Chaim, who was an old-fashioned rabbi and didn't know much about worldly things.

"What do you do," asked Reb Chaim, "when someone asks you to decide whether a particular item is kosher or not?"

"I always decide it's not kosher," answered the rabbi.

"Let me tell you a story," said Reb Chaim.

> There once was an agricultural leaseholder who lived out in the country, far from town. In the winter he used to slaughter geese for their fat, as country folk do. From time to time he'd have a question about whether a certain goose was kosher. Since there was no rabbi nearby, he always had to harness up his horse and ride to town to get his questions answered.
>
> One time a certain Jew who was a bit of a wise guy happened to stop at the leaseholder's inn. The leaseholder complained that he'd had many ques-

tions about kashrus that winter, and it was terribly inconvenient to have to ride to town every time.

"I have some advice for you," said the guest. "The Torah says: *l'kelev tashlichun oso,* 'throw it to the dog.' That means that nonkosher food belongs to dogs. So any time you have doubts about the kashrus of a goose, you should place it in front of a dog. If he eats it—it's not kosher, but if he refuses it—it's kosher."

The leaseholder was very pleased at the idea that he wouldn't have to go ask the rabbi every time he had a question.

A few days later he slaughtered a goose, and he wasn't sure if it was kosher. The leaseholder placed the goose in front of a dog, and everybody in the household stood around to see whether the dog would eat it or not. The dog sniffed at the goose with great interest, but seeing all the people standing around him, was too scared to touch it.

"Kosher! Kosher!" Everybody was happy, and they ate the goose.

But as the dog became used to having everybody standing around him, any time a goose was placed before it, he would eat the whole thing and not leave a scrap behind.

Now things weren't looking so good for the leaseholder. The next time he had a question, he didn't rely on the dog, and instead he went to town to ask the rabbi.

The rabbi asked, "How come I haven't seen you for so long? You're not slaughtering geese anymore? Not a single question came up?"

"No, rabbi," answered the leaseholder. "I have geese, and questions come up, but until now my dog was able to rule on them."

"And now?" asked the rabbi.

"Now, rabbi," sighed the leaseholder, "the dog always decides they're not kosher."

57

When Reb Mordche Aren Ginsburg passed away in Vilna, the local Maskilim, proponents of the Jewish Enlightenment, approached Reb Velvele, the community Maggid, to see if he would be willing to eulogize Reb Mordche. At first Reb Velvele, who was a well-known and committed opponent of the Maskilim, refused. But they were insistent, and since he didn't want to have an open dispute with them, he agreed to do the eulogy.

He came up with a way to solve his predicament. Just at that time, two rabbis from small towns near Vilna had died. Reb Velvele devoted his entire eulogy to the two small-town rabbis, citing verses from Torah and Talmudic sayings to underscore the great loss to the Jewish people and moving the audience to tears. Finally he mentioned that Mordche Aren Ginsburg had also died, and he managed to say a few nice things about him to be polite. The Vilna Maskilim deeply resented this.

After the funeral, Adam Hacohen approached Reb Velvele and said, "Maggid, your eulogy helped me understand a verse in the Torah. The person who came to inform King David that Jonathan and Saul had died is called a 'na'ar,' a 'lad' in Hebrew. But 'nar' means 'fool' in Yiddish! So what was foolish about him? Your eulogy answered my question. He did just the same thing you did. He said, 'The men fled from the battle. Many of them fell and died. And Saul and his son Jonathan are dead.' The real loss—the death of Saul and Jonathan—he only mentioned at the end, in passing. That kind of Maggid is a fool."

Reb Velvele listened quietly and then replied: "I'll tell you a story."

A merchant from Vilna who conducted business in foreign countries once married off a child. He invited a good friend of his to the wedding, a merchant from Königsberg with whom he'd done business for years. The wedding jester was Yitschok Smargoner, who was brilliant at making rhymes that played on the numerical value of the names of the bride and groom and their parents. The merchant from Königsberg enjoyed the jester's performance immensely.

Some time later, the merchant from Königsberg married off a child of his own. He brought Yitschok Smargoner to entertain the families of the couple. But this time the performance failed. Yitschok Smargoner couldn't open his mouth. He tried playing around with gematria, but nothing came out right. All he could come up with were a few clichéd rhymes. The merchant from Königsberg was perplexed. He approached the jester and demanded in German: 'Herr Jester, what happened to you?'

'It's like this,' answered Yitschok Smargoner. 'Usually when I'm hired for a wedding, the groom is named Avrom or Moyshe; the bride is Esther or Miriam. And it's the same with their close relatives. I know how to work in the numerical values of those names. But this is the first time I've been at a wedding where the groom is named Heinrich, the bride is Gertrude, and the family members are Ignatz, Moritz, Bertha, Frieda. I don't even know how to spell such names. So I can't do anything with their numerical values. You'll see, when I have more such weddings, I'll get used to these German names, and I'll do fine.'

"With me it's the same," concluded Reb Velvele. "I'm used to eulogizing saints, rabbis, and respectable Jews. So I know how to approach them. This is the first time I've had to eulogize a Maskil, and it's no surprise that it didn't go well. You'll see, when I eulogize more of them, I'll get used to it and I'll do fine."

58

When the state-sponsored rabbinical seminary in Vilna first opened, its trustees asked Reb Yisroel Salanter, who was then the rosh yeshiva in Vilna, to serve as the government's official inspector for the new seminary. Reb Yisroel wouldn't even consider it. The trustees petitioned the government officials to convince Reb Yisroel to accept the position. Reb Yisroel found out about this and left town for a while, and Hirsh Katzenellenbogen was named the inspector instead.

Years later, Dr. Shafir from Kovno asked Reb Yisroel, "Tell me, Rabbi, why didn't you want to take the position in the rabbinical seminary? It seems to me that if that institution were under your supervision, it would be more Jewish and would produce rabbis who are learned in both Torah and secular subjects."

"Let me ask you something," answered Reb Yisroel. "We see that when a poor person comes to a rabbi to ask whether a piece of meat he bought is not kosher, the rabbi stops what he's doing and immediately answers. If it's a difficult question, he thinks it over, researches the matter, and tries to find ways to rule that the item is indeed kosher, so that the poor person won't suffer. But when the rich person asks the same questions, the rabbi isn't in such a rush, and he's not so determined to find a way to rule it kosher.

"A doctor is the opposite. He runs to go treat a rich man, but when he's summoned to a pauper's bedside, he comes up with all kinds of excuses not to go. And if he does end up going, he drags his feet the entire way.

"So why is it, do you think, that rabbis prefer poor people while doctors prefer the rich?" continued Reb Yisroel. "It's like this," he explained. "A rabbi doesn't study in order to become a rabbi. He studies because that's what a Jew is supposed to do. As he studies, he becomes imbued with the ethics of Torah, which is completely based in justice and righteousness—that is, helping the poor and oppressed. And if he happens to become a rabbi later on, he continues to be guided by the same ethics.

"But a doctor starts out studying with the goal of becoming a doctor. He doesn't go to university out of a sense of compassion, in order to be able to heal the sick. He studies medicine because it's a good way to make a living and be respected in society. And that's why when he does become a doctor, he'd rather have a rich patient who can provide him with money and status.

"The rabbinical seminary came along," Reb Yisroel concluded, "and wanted to turn the rabbinate into a proper profession, a path for young men to go make a living. Such rabbis will be just like doctors. They'll flatter the rich and avoid the poor. That's why I refused to have anything to do with it."

64

[The Yiddish word taytsh *can mean either a German (here, a Jew dressed in "German," that is modern, style) or an interpretation of a Biblical phrase. The latter sense stems from the former—the set of words used for everyday translation of the Torah into Yiddish was once called "Ivri-taytsh," "Hebrew-German." Meanwhile, the Hebrew words* dovor akher *(literally "something else") can mean either "another interpretation" or, as a euphemism, "pig" or even "Satan."]*

Reb Ayzl Kharif was sitting in a train. With him in the compartment sat two young men, modern types, *taytshn*. One of them made fun of Reb Ayzl, who wore old-fashioned clothes like a rabbi of yesteryear. The older Jews in the compartment resented this.

"Why are you surprised?" Reb Ayzl called over to them. "You must have studied Rashi's Biblical commentary, so you know that wherever there are two *taytshn*, interpretations, Rashi calls the second one a *dover akher*, a pig."

68

Reb Shneur Zalmen of Liadi once paid a visit to a worldly rabbi who bitterly opposed Hasidism. The latter asked him, "Please tell me: Who is this Elimelech fellow who wrote a book called *Noam Elimelech*? I've got that book right under the bench here, on the floor."

"You want to know who Reb Elimelech is? I'll tell you: Even if you put Reb Elimelech Lizhensker himself under the bench, it wouldn't bother him and you'd never hear him complain."

69

Reb Chaim Volozhiner, a disciple of the Vilna Gaon, sharply opposed Hasidism and what he saw as the Hasidic tendency to impose spiritual readings onto the plain text of the Torah.

A Hasidic rabbi once came to visit him. Reb Chaim greeted him cordially and ordered refreshments to be set out as for a welcome guest. Naturally, as they were eating, they spoke words of Torah. The Hasidic rabbi recalled a liturgical phrase from the concluding Yom Kippur prayer service: "*Ezkera elokim v'ehemaye be're'osi kol ir al tilo bnuyo; v'ir ha'elokim mushpeles ad she'oyl takhtis.*" The rabbi gave a phrase-by-phrase homiletic interpretation:

"*Ezkera elokim v'ehemaye be're'osi kol ir*: When it says 'ir,' city, what it really means is material attachment, all the worldly passions. They are *al tilo bnuyo*, in the supernal sphere.

"And when it says, *v'ir ha'elokim*, the Divine City, it really means all spiritual longing, the passion for Divine service, which is *mushpeles ad she'oyl takhtis*, sadly in a lowly state."

Reb Chaim listened to the Hasidic rabbi's Torah in silence. After a long pause, he asked:

"Have you ever been to St. Petersburg?"

"No!" answered the guest.

"But you've heard of St. Petersburg?"

"Yes," answered the guest, "of course I've heard of it."

"St. Petersburg is a large city, with long, wide avenues, with large, beautiful buildings, with palaces and gardens—you can't take your eyes off it."

The Hasidic rabbi listened and wondered why Reb Chaim was speaking of such trivial matters, singing the praises of a Gentile city.

"And have you ever been to Warsaw? Warsaw is also a beautiful city, with paved streets and buildings made of stone."

The guest stared at him.

"They say," continued Reb Chaim, "that Berlin is a beautiful city, that it's really something. Not to mention Paris!"

The Hasidic rabbi couldn't restrain himself any longer. "Yes, but why... "

"Oh, I thought you might have been confused about what 'ir' means," Reb Chaim innocently replied, knowing full well the Hasidic rabbi knew the Hebrew word for "city." "Here is what that verse means: 'kol ir: every city—for example St. Petersburg, Warsaw, Berlin, Paris—al tilo bnuyo: stands intact. V'ir ha'elokim—and the Divine City, Jerusalem—mushpeles ad she'oyl takhtis, is laid low, ruined and empty.'"

73

A Karliner Hasid was once on his way to see the Rebbe in Karlin. As he was passing through Antipolye, he stopped to see the rabbi, Reb Pinches Michl, who was a renowned scholar and a perfect saint—yet an opponent of Hasidism. Reb Pinches Michl warmly welcomed the Hasid and started a conversation with him: "So, where are you from? And where are you heading?"

The Hasid answered that he was from such-and-such a place, and was on his way to Karlin to see his rebbe.

"In order to see a rebbe," asked Reb Pinches Michl in his humble way, "do you really need to travel all the way to Karlin?"

"I am a clairvoyant," answered the Hasid, "and I can tell that there isn't a true rebbe to be found until Karlin."

"Really?" wondered Reb Pinches Michl. "A clairvoyant, are you?

So please, do me a favor: Tell me what I'm thinking right now."

Without hesitation, the Hasid responded, "You're thinking of the verse *shevisi hashem kinegdi tomid*, 'I have set the Lord before me always.'"

"You guessed wrong," said Reb Pinches Michl. "Just now I was thinking something different."

"And that's exactly why," triumphantly replied the Hasid, "no one travels to see you!"

76

Reb Yoshe Ber Brisker used to say: "Those Hasidic rebbes have messed up the Jewish masses so badly that now we actually need them."

78

Leyzer Yashinovker, Nisn Rozental's father, was known as the biggest heretic in all Lithuania.

When he was on his deathbed, he summoned his son and said, "Listen to me, Nisn. Your older brother has converted, so he won't say kaddish for me. Your sisters have no obligation to say kaddish.

"You are the only one left. I'm begging you—don't you say kaddish either!"

79

On his deathbed, Leyzer Yashinovker asked for a wormy plum to eat, which isn't kosher.

"Why do you want that?" they asked.

"If they're going to whip me in the World to Come for my sins in this one," answered Leyzer, "I'll have no idea when they'll be finished: I have so many sins! This way, when they get around to whipping me for the wormy plum, at least I'll know that the whipping is finally done."

84

[This anecdote relies on a Hebrew pun of the root n-ts-r, which can mean either "be created" or "become Christian."]

Even after his conversion to Christianity, Professor Daniel Chwolson thought of himself as a Jew. He would intervene with the authorities in St. Petersburg on behalf of the Jews. And when he corresponded with the greatest rabbis of his generation, such as Reb Yitschok Elchonon, Reb Hersh Leyb, Reb Dovid Karliner, and other luminaries, he always referred to "us Jews."

When the Russian Empire banned traditional Jewish schooling, Reb Yitschok Elchonon wrote to Chwolson, asking him to intervene to have the decree revoked. He quoted the Mishnaic phrase in his letter, *ki le-khakh noytsarto,* meaning in its original context, "for such a purpose, *noytsarto*—you were created," but meaning here, "for such a purpose, *nutsarto*—you converted."

But Chwolson didn't think much of his chances. He quoted from the Yom Kippur liturgy: *Ad she-loy noytsarti eyni kiday ve-akhshov she-noytsarti ke-ielu loy noytsarti,* which in that context means: "Until *noytsarti*—I was created—I was unfit to exist, and now that *noytsarti*—I have been created—in the eyes of God I am like one who was never created at all." But here he meant, "until *nutsarti*—I converted—I was unfit to intervene, and now that *nutsarti*—I have converted—in the eyes of the government, it's still as if I never became Christian at all."

88

The government censor of Jewish publications in St. Petersburg, Zusman, was a convert to Christianity. His Jewish literacy was profound, and he enjoyed discussing matters of Torah with religious and secular Jewish scholars. But he had a weakness for drink.

One time he went out for a stroll on Nevsky Prospect with the Jewish writer Koyfman and they discussed matters of Torah. They passed by a tavern and went in. Zusman ordered a large glass of liquor, crossed himself, and slugged it down in one swallow.

Koyfman stared at him.

"No doubt you're surprised," said Zusman. "Here I was discussing Torah with you, and now I've made the sign of the cross. It's like this. You see, I know I look like a Jew. I don't want the Gentiles around us to think that Jews are drunkards."

592

A German pastor was once arguing matters of faith with Moses Mendelssohn.

"If you believe in the Father," said the pastor, "you must believe in the Son as well. That's how the world is: People give a rich man's son just as much credit as they give his father."

"Yes," retorted Mendelssohn, "but not the kind of son whose father will live forever!"

593

Although Reb Zalmen Poyzner was a Jewish aristocrat, he dressed in a very simple and old-fashioned manner, as was common in those days. He wore a sable shtreiml. It was extremely valuable. A Polish nobleman with whom he was acquainted once accosted him: "How come you wear such simple and cheap clothes, and such an expensive shtreiml on your head?"

"I'll tell you, Your Grace," Reb Zalmen answered him, "for you the body is the main thing, so you clothe it in the most expensive garments. But the head isn't so important, so you leave it bare. With us Jews, it's the opposite. The body isn't so important to us, so we'll put on any old garment. But for us, the head is the main thing, so we dress it as well as we can."

594

When Reb Zalmen Poyzner lived on his estate at Kuchar, he wanted to train Jews in agricultural work. He took a number of Jewish families, settled them on his land, gave them plots of land, and turned them into peasants.

Once, he and Reb Shayele Kutner went out to the fields to watch the Jewish peasants working. It was the plowing season. On one side Gentile peasants were working their fields, and on the other side Jews were plowing theirs.

"You see," said Reb Zalmen, "Gentiles are plowing, and Jews— *lehavdil*—are plowing. These people are praying, and those other people are also praying. The Gentiles pray for a good harvest: rain should fall at the right time and in the right amount, the grain should sprout, the cutting should go well, the corn crib should be full, and so on. What do Jews pray for? Everyone prays for himself: 'O Master of the Universe, may my plow uncover a buried treasure, so that I can stop this backbreaking labor already!'"

598

Once a prominent French government minister died. All of the leading officials, led by the president, participated in the funeral. Reb Tsadok Kahn, the chief rabbi of France, also attended the funeral.

The funeral cortege passed through a Jewish cemetery on the way to the Gentile cemetery. Since he was a Kohen—belonging to the priestly class—and forbidden to enter a Jewish cemetery, Reb Tsadok walked all the way around it until he reached the Gentile cemetery and stood by the grave.

The president asked him, "Why, Monsieur Rabbi, did you avoid the Jewish cemetery?"

"I am a Kohen," answered Reb Tsadok, "and Jewish law forbids a Kohen from entering a cemetery."

The president asked further, "Then why did you go to the Gentile cemetery? Aren't Gentiles people, too?"

"I'll tell you, Mr. President," answered Reb Tsadok. "Your Jesus said that he wouldn't die, and nobody who believed in him would die, so your graves don't make us impure. Our Moses said that he would die, and then he died. We Jews all die, so Jewish graves make us impure."

607

Reb Mordche Boysker loved to talk about the Holy Land, how wonderful it would be when the Jews would return there to dwell once again, each "under his vine and fig tree."

"Rebbe," someone once asked him, "what about the Temple sacrifices? Will we really sacrifice cattle like in the old days? It's hard to imagine."

"Ay, Reb Yid!" sighed Reb Mordche. "If you knew just how many problems we have to overcome before we live to see that holy hour, you'd know you can leave that particular problem for later."

610

Around the time Eliezer Ben Yehuda began speaking the Holy Tongue as his everyday language, he once went to visit Reb Shmuel Moliver. Reb Shmuel warmly welcomed Ben Yehuda and invited him to sit down. Ben Yehuda opened his mouth and started speaking Hebrew. Reb Shmuel listened, but he barely understood one word in ten. He tried to respond, but he couldn't get his tongue around the words. Very few people spoke Hebrew back then.

A while passed with Ben Yehuda talking and Reb Shmuel barely saying a word.

Eventually Reb Shmuel spoke up. "Listen, young man. Drop this foolish affectation and talk like a normal person!"

612

Dr. Yitzchok Dembo, who was famous for his lobbying to make sure that kosher slaughter wouldn't be banned in Russia, went to the Zionist Congress in Basel.

When he returned, someone asked him: "Doctor, what did you do at the Zionist Congress?"

"I went," Dembo smiled, "to lobby to make sure that if there will be a Jewish state, they won't ban kosher slaughter there, either."

615

After the poet Chaim Nachman Bialik moved to the Land of Israel, he once went to meet a merchant about a business deal. Bialik began the conversation in Yiddish.

"What, Mr. Bialik," the merchant reproached him. "Why are you, of all people, not speaking Hebrew?"

"No problem," responded Bialik, "if you've got the time, we can speak Hebrew."

618

Once Reb Zalmen Poyzner was riding in his coach-and-four. A Hasid was riding with him. Some Gentile boys started chasing after them, mockingly shouting "*Zhid!*" The Hasid sighed deeply, hoping to ingratiate himself with Reb Zalmen.

"No need to sigh," smiled Reb Zalmen. "When Moshiach comes, *they'll* be the ones in exile; they'll ride around in coaches while *we* chase after *them*."

624

In 1798, when Reb Shneur Zalmen was imprisoned for the first time in the Peter-Paul Fortress of St. Petersburg, he was allowed no visitors. But eventually the warden was "persuaded" to allow his close associate Reb Shoyel Siratshiner to come.

Once while Reb Shoyel was visiting the Rav in his cell, the warden of the prison rushed into the room in a panic. "Rabbi, we are done for! The Tsar himself is coming to visit you. He's already on the way in. What am I going to do about that Jew who's with you? Where can I hide him? There's only one door out!"

"Don't be afraid," said Reb Shneur Zalmen. "The Tsar won't see this Jew."

"What will you do?" asked the warden.

"You'll find out later," said Reb Shneur Zalmen. "Now go in good spirits."

The warden shrugged his shoulders and left.

When the warden had gone, Reb Shneur Zalmen told Reb Shoyel to stand by the window, and lowered the drape in front of him.

The Tsar came in and sat with the Rav for several hours, asking him all kinds of questions. Reb Shoyel stood stock-still by the window behind the drape the entire time.

When the Tsar left, the warden ran back in and saw Reb Shoyel sitting with the Rav. "Where were you while the Tsar was here?" he asked.

"Here," answered Reb Shoyel.

"And he didn't see you?" the warden asked further.

"No," said Reb Shoyel.

The warden stared at the Rav and at Reb Shoyel in amazement. "Well, one of you must certainly be a wizard."

"No," said the Rav. "He was standing right here by the window, behind the drape."

"That was quite the gamble," said the warden. "What would you have done if the Tsar had opened the drape? You would have been a dead man."

"Well, it was only logical," said the Rav. "Etiquette certainly forbids the great Tsar from getting up to draw open the drape."

627

In 1843, the Russian government convened a conference in St. Petersburg to reform Jewish education. While there, Reb Itsele Volozhiner made a very strong impression on the Russian educational minister Sergei Uvarov, author of the new Russian doctrine of "Orthodoxy, Autocracy, and Nationality."

Uvarov once remarked to Reb Itsele with great condescension, "You know, Rabbi, if you devoted your mind to secular education rather than Talmud, you could be a minister."

"And you, my lord minister," replied Reb Itsele, "if you devoted yourself to Talmud, you could be a rabbi!"

630

In the 18th century, Jews in the Austro-Hungarian Empire weren't allowed to own their own drugstores. Yoysef Perl, one of the first Maskilim in Galicia, who enjoyed the personal favor of Emperor Josef II, sent his son to study pharmacy and received permission from the emperor to open a drugstore. When everyone in the emperor's court heard about this, there was an uproar: What madness is this? A Jew running a drugstore? All of the ministers met and decided to petition the emperor to revoke the license.

The emperor sent for Perl and said to him:

"The court is in a frenzy. All of my ministers are outraged. But I can't revoke the license I gave you. Please be so kind as to renounce it voluntarily. In return, I'll give you whatever you want, 'up to half my kingdom.'"

"Very well," said Perl. "My request is this: that the emperor return to my son the years he wasted studying pharmacy."

"That," replied the emperor, "is something no human being can give."

"Since even the emperor himself can't give someone everything he desires, neither should he take back what he once gave."

And Perl had his way. His son became a pharmacist.

635

During the reign of Alexander III, there was a government minister named Ignatiev who issued one anti-Jewish decree after another. It was rumored in St. Petersburg that a group of Jews led by Baron Ginzburg were raising money to bribe Ignatiev.

Ignatiev ran into Baron Ginzburg, as occasionally happened.

"I've heard," he said to the Baron with a smile, "that you're raising money for me. How much were you thinking?"

"Lord Minister," answered the Baron, "What I think Jews are worth, I could never pay you. But what *you* think Jews are worth, I'm always ready to hand over."

637

Reb Hirsh, the Rabbi of Berlin, was once asked, "Tell us, Rabbi, why is it that today's Maskilim are completely irreligious? There were reformers in earlier times as well. They studied philosophy and science but remained faithful Jews."

"It's like this," responded Reb Hirsh. "When an old-time reformer studied philosophy and science, he would sit and study all day long until he had mastered each topic. If he studied *The Guide to the Perplexed*, he understood the metaphysical problem that Maimonides posed and understood how Maimonides solved it. As a result, his faith was actually strengthened.

"But your contemporary Maskil is busy all day long with other things. At night before he goes to sleep, he takes a glance at the *Guide*. He has just enough time to become engrossed in Maimonides' problem before he falls asleep. He never gets to Maimonides' solution, and so he's left with a head full of doubts."

642

A wise-guy reformer once asked the Malbim, "Rebbe, I have a tough question for you. We know that when we see a rabbi, we're supposed to stand up. When we see a dog, we're supposed to sit down. What do we do when we see a rabbi and a dog?"

"There's really no established rule," answered the Malbim. "It depends on local custom. Why don't we go out into the marketplace, you and I, and see what the people do?"

646

In Reb Ayzl Kharif's day, people started wearing short jackets with a pocket sewn high up on the breast.

"It saddens me," sighed Red Ayzl, "to see how small Jews have become."

"What do you mean, Rebbe?" someone asked.

"It's like this," answered Reb Ayzl. "There's a saying: 'He's a Jew all the way down to his pockets.' Now the pocket is very high, and the Jew, alas, is very small."

651

Reb Hersh Leyb Volozhiner was close friends with Chaim Zelig Slonimsky and corresponded with him regularly, even though Slonimsky was a somewhat infamous reformer.

When the Volozhin yeshiva was shut down by the Russian government in 1892, Reb Hersh Leyb moved to Warsaw, where he was warmly received and respected by Hasidim and more modern Jews alike. Rabbis, scholars, and reformers came to talk to him about matters of Torah and current events. Slonimsky, who was by that time over eighty, never went to see Reb Hersh Leyb. Everyone in his circle found this odd, but they chalked it up to Slonimsky's advanced age. Or perhaps, they speculated, Slonimsky didn't know that Reb Hersh Leyb was in Warsaw.

One time, one of Reb Hersh Leyb's associates asked him directly: "Reb Chaim Zelig, do you know that Reb Hersh Leyb is living in Warsaw?"

"Yes," nodded Slonimsky, "I know."

"Why is that you haven't gone to visit him? Is there some dispute between you?"

"God forbid!" said Slonimsky. "I am a true and loyal friend of his, and that's exactly why I don't go to see him."

The questioner stared back at him. Was Slonimsky senile?

"Here's how it is," explained Slonimsky. "I know the Hasidim in Warsaw. If they see me visiting Reb Hersh Leyb, they'll completely ostracize him. They consider me to be a heretic, a traitor to Judaism, and if Reb Hersh Leyb is friendly with me, they'll think he's no better. And I know that right now Reb Hersh Leyb needs their support. That's why I stay away."

652

Reb Alexander Moyshe Lapidus, the Rabbi of Raseyn, was once riding in a train. Together with him in the car were a group of young wise guys who decided to make fun of the old-fashioned rabbi.

"Rebbe," they said, "we have a question for you."

"Yes?" asked Reb Alexander Moyshe.

"We want to kiss the mezuzah, but there isn't a mezuzah in the train."

"In that case," answered Reb Alexander Moyshe, "you can go kiss something else."

653

Reb Samson Raphael Hirsch, the Rabbi of Frankfurt, had a saying: "Since rabbis began calling themselves 'doctors,' Judaism has grown sick."

656

In his old age, Shmuel Yoysef Fuenn returned to a traditional Jewish life and observed the ritual laws, as was befitting a trustee of the communal charity bureau. But people whispered all over town that he still wasn't religious: once a Maskil, always a Maskil.

Fuenn once complained, "You know, there are days when I recite minchah five times. What do I mean? Well, at 12:30 pm the secretary of the gravediggers' synagogue comes in and tells me they're getting ready to recite minchah early, so I put everything aside and follow him.

"A half hour later the rest of the trustees, Yerachmiel Broyde and Yankev Parnes, come into the office. There are always paupers at the bureau, so there's a minyan. Broyde says we should recite minchah, so who am I to tell him I've already prayed? He wouldn't believe me, so I do it again.

"When I'm done at the office, I head home toward the Snipishok neighborhood. As I'm walking down the German Street, the secretary of the Free Loan Society synagogue—an honest Jew—spots me and calls out: 'Reb Shmuel Yosl, we're getting ready to pray! By the time you get home it will be rather late.'

"So I go in and pray a third time.

"As I reach the Green Bridge, a Jew grabs my arm: 'Reb Shmuel Yosl, there are mourners sitting shiva here, may we be spared, and we need one more to make the minyan. Please be so kind as to help us out.'

"What can I do? I go in and pray a fourth time.

"Then, when I've finally dragged myself home to Snipishok, the secretary of the synagogue there pops out and says, 'Reb Shmuel Yosl, everybody's waiting for you to start minchah.'

"So I go in and do it for the fifth time. What choice do I have?"

Once someone told this story to Reb Shimen Strashun. "Don't believe that Maskil," he replied. "He doesn't pray even once."

661

Shomer, the famous writer of Yiddish romance novels, paid a visit to Kalisz. He went to see the rabbi, Reb Chaim Elozer Vaks. Reb Chaim Elozer greeted him, invited him to sit down, and struck up a conversation.

"So, where are you from? What do you do?"

"I am a Yiddish writer," answered Shomer.

"What monographs have you published?" asked Reb Chaim Elozer.

"I write novels," answered Shomer. "I've published dozens already. I've just published a new one called *The Spiteful Apostate*."

"What a pity," said Reb Chaim Elozer. "You're writing your own epitaph, and it's a bad one."

"What do you mean, Rabbi?"

"I'll tell you," responded Reb Chaim Elozer. "You know that we Jews have the custom of referring to the author by the name of his book, and to write on the gravestone: Here lies the *Magen Avraham*,

The Shield of Abraham; the *Pnei Yehoshua*, The Face of Joshua; the *Pri Megodim*, The Luscious Fruits. On your gravestone they'll write: Here lies *Der Meshumed Lehakhes*, The Spiteful Apostate."

667

Reb Itsele Volozhiner bitterly opposed Hasidism and didn't respect the Hasidic wonder rabbis. That was the Volozhiner way.

Reb Itsele was once at a social gathering when the topic of Hasidic rabbis came up. He interjected, "Gentlemen, you know the difference between the title 'The Brilliant Rabbi,' which one uses for one of our rabbis, and 'The Holy Light,' which the Hasidim call their rebbes? 'The Brilliant Rabbi' is headache, and 'The Holy Light' is stomachache."

"What do you mean, Rebbe?" they asked him.

Reb Itsele explained: "If a child doesn't want to go to school, he pretends to be sick. A simple child says, 'Mommy, I have a headache.'

"The mother feels his head, and she can tell right away if he's really sick or just pretending. If he doesn't have a fever, she makes him go to school.

"A clever child says, 'Mommy, my stomach hurts.'

"What can the mother do? She has to believe the child.

"Same thing here," Reb Itsele concluded. "If someone calls himself 'Brilliant Rabbi,' you can feel his head, ask him a couple of good questions, and you know right away whether he's really brilliant or just pretending. But if someone calls himself 'Holy Light,' you just have to believe it."

669

A Misnagid once said to Reb Yisroel Rizhiner: "You see the difference, Rebbe, between Misnagdim and Hasidim. Misnagdim go and study Mishnah after praying, while Hasidim go and drink liquor."

"Well, it stands to reason," answered the Rizhiner. "The Misnagdim pray as if they're dead, and it's customary to study Mishnah after someone dies. The Hasidim are lively when they pray, and if you're alive and breathing, you need a drink."

675

Reb Zalmen Poyzner used to say: "I don't know why all the Hasidim hate me so much. If I talk to a Kotsker Hasid, he tells me the Izhbitser Rebbe is totally worthless. If I talk to an Izhbitser Hasid, he only has nasty things to say about the Kotsker Rebbe. And that's how it is with Hasidim—each one claims the other rebbe's no good. So what's their problem with me, if I happen to agree with all of them?"

682

There was a rich Jew named Moyshe Rozenson who lived in Vilna. He was a notorious Christian missionary. He printed books supposedly proving that the Nazirite was the Messiah, and he would distribute them free of charge. Everybody in Vilna knew better than to have anything to do with him or his books.

Rozenson once complained, "It's so frustrating. I left the books out by the kitchen window, hoping that a poor man would break in and steal them. But he breaks in, steals a silver spoon, and doesn't touch the books."

683

The apostate Jacob Brafman, whose *Kahal Book* encouraged terrible antisemitism, was a total ignoramus. His malicious, slapdash "research" was either purchased from poor Talmud scholars or based on books he could barely make his way through.

One time, Brafman entered the Imperial Library in St. Petersburg and asked Harkavy, the chief librarian, if he could consult the volumes titled *Ibid* and *Ibidem*. Since he'd seen them cited practically everywhere, they must be very important works.

Harkavy answered with a straight face that those volumes weren't available at the moment, but he would do his best to obtain them.

"I apologize for the inconvenience," he said as he handed a card to Brafman. "Please write down that you're requesting these titles, and sign at the bottom."

Brafman did so without hesitation: He wrote down and signed that he was looking for the books *Ibid* and *Ibidem*.

Harkavy showed the card to all the newspapers, and everyone in St. Petersburg was soon talking about Brafman's humiliation.

Clergy and Community

90

[*Va'ad Arba'Aratzos (The Council of Four Lands) was the central body of Jewish authority in the Polish-Lithuanian Commonwealth from the second half of the 16th century to 1764.*]

The Vilna Gaon had made an agreement with the trustees of the community that he was not to be summoned to a meeting unless it involved a proposed new communal regulation.

The trustees once wanted to pass a regulation stating that no outside paupers would be admitted to Vilna. They called a meeting and sent for the Gaon to join them.

The Gaon came. When he heard what the question was, he said to the trustees: "We had an agreement that you wouldn't summon me to a meeting unless it had to do with a new regulation."

"Yes, Rabbi," they responded, "this is a new regulation that we're proposing."

"No," said the Gaon, "it's an old regulation, established long ago by the Council of Four Lands."

"The Four Lands?" wondered the trustees. "We didn't know about that. The record books of the Council of Four Lands mention no such regulation."

"Not today's Four Lands," said the Gaon. "The ones from long ago: 'Sodom, Gemorah, Admah, and Tsvoyim, which God overthrew in his anger and in his wrath.' They, too, had a regulation forbidding the admission of any paupers."

93

The Sanz study house employed a secretary, Ruvn was his name, and people whispered in town that he was less than careful with the community funds. There were several attempts to get him fired. But Reb Chaim, the Sanzer Rebbe, always intervened on his behalf.

A rich man from Russia once visited Sanz and contributed 100 rubles to the study house. Ruvn took the money and pocketed it. People in the community found out and ran to Reb Chaim, crying, "It's a scandal! How can you let him get away with it?"

Reb Chaim answered, "You should know that there's a special throne in Gan Eden reserved for secretaries who deal honestly with communal funds. To this day, that chair remains empty. Not a single secretary has ever sat on it. And you expect Ruvn to be the first?"

94

There was a government informer among the Jews in Slonim. Any time something came up in the community that the authorities didn't need to know, the community would pay the informer hush money.

There once arose a tricky situation that would have been very damaging to the community if it were leaked. The informer demanded an enormous sum in return for his silence, three hundred rubles. Reb Ayzl Kharif convened a meeting to discuss what to do. They sent for the informer and tried to bargain with him, but he wouldn't budge. Three hundred rubles and not a penny less. And if not, he would inform the authorities.

"You gangster, you brat!" shouted Reb Ayzl. "Take fifity—now that's a fair price. And if not, the community will go find us another informer who'll keep quiet for twenty-five!"

96

Reb Yoshe Ber Brisker had a secretary for his rabbinical court whom the trustees of the community didn't like. They called a meeting and resolved to fire the secretary. They told Reb Yoshe Ber to convey the news to the secretary, but Reb Yoshe Ber didn't want to do it.

"Why not, rabbi? You're the rabbi, and he's your secretary."

"Here's how it is," answered Reb Yoshe Ber. "Every day in our morning prayers, we recite the story of the binding of Isaac. So you know that when God told Abraham to bring Isaac as a sacrifice, He conveyed the instructions Himself. It is explicitly written: *va-yoymer kakh no es binkho es yekhidkho*—and [God] said, 'Take your son, your only son.' Yet when God wanted Abraham to stop, to spare Isaac, he sent an angel, as it is written: *va-yikro eylov malakh hashem el avrohom*—and an angel of God called to Abraham.

"So this raises a question: Why didn't God send the angel in the first place? The answer is: God knew that no angel would have complied. Each of them would have said, 'If You want to kill a Jew, go give the order yourself.'"

101

When Reb Yeshaya Horowitz, the rabbi of Frankfurt, passed away, he left a will stipulating that whoever could solve a certain set of three problems in the field of Torah should be his successor.

The community sent three scholarly community trustees to travel around the world until they found a great man worthy of occupying the rabbinic seat. The emissaries went from city to city until they arrived in Krakow, which has always been a city full of Torah scholars.

Soon all of Krakow was buzzing with the arrival of the emissaries from Frankfurt. It happened that on that very day, one of the wealthy members of the community was having his baby son circumcised, and he invited the guests to the ceremony.

During the ensuing feast, the rich man's older son gave a lecture on Torah that his teacher had prepared for him. In the middle of the lecture, the emissaries from Frankfurt were astonished: The boy had solved all three problems.

They asked, "Who is the lad's teacher?"

The answer came, "Reb Yoysef Shmuel, the president of the society *"Shomrim Laboker,"* Watchers of the Morning—sitting there at the end of the table."

The Jews from Frankfurt approached him and with deep humility requested a private audience with him to discuss an important matter.

"I'm a schoolteacher," answered Reb Yoysef Shmuel, "and I can't waste my time."

But the emissaries wouldn't leave him alone until he agreed to hear them out.

When Reb Yoysef Shmuel heard that they wanted to appoint him as rabbi of Frankfurt, he stared at them and shook his head. "How can I be the rabbi of Frankfurt? I'm just a simple teacher."

The emissaries explained about Reb Yeshaya's will and begged him with all their might to accept the position, arguing this way and that—but to no avail. Reb Yoysef Shmuel was entirely unwilling to accept a rabbinical position. The emissaries left town empty-handed.

Eight days later Reb Yoysef Shmuel fell sick. As he lay on his sickbed, he raised his eyes and said, "Master of the Universe, if You really want me to go to Frankfurt, I will submit my will to Your own."

Reb Yoysef Shmuel became the rabbi of Frankfurt, and he grew famous for his brilliant scholarship and righteous ways.

102

Reb Avrom Abish, the rabbi of Frankfurt, decreed on his deathbed that Reb Oyzer of Klementov, the author of *Even Oyzer*, should be named his successor.

After the shiva, the communal leaders of Frankfurt traveled to Klementov with a letter of appointment to the Frankfurt rabbinate.

They got to the rabbi's house and the door was open. They walked inside, but nobody was there. So they went out into the courtyard and saw the rabbi's wife milking a goat, with the rabbi standing nearby.

When Reb Oyzer noticed these unknown guests, he came over, and warmly greeted them and invited them into the house. They went in, told him about Reb Avrom Abish's decree, and showed him the letter of appointment.

"Why should I go to Frankfurt?" said Reb Oyzer. "Am I lacking anything, God forbid, here in Klementov? You see how it is. I have a goat, and thank God, I get by. Maybe one day I'll have two goats—then I'll really be living in style!"

103

Reb Shmelke traveled to Nikolsburg to assume the post of town rabbi. The whole town went out to greet and honor him.

As soon as he arrived, Reb Shmelke asked the crowd to let him spend a little while in a room by himself. Everyone thought this was a little bit odd: The new rabbi already needs to be by himself? But no one said a word.

One of the townspeople, however, was curious to see what Reb Shmelke was doing. He put his ear to the door and heard Reb Shmelke talking to himself: "Welcome, Rabbi of Nikolsburg! Greetings, Rabbi! Sit down, Reb Shmelke."

He couldn't believe his ears.

Later, when Reb Shmelke had come outside to join the crowd, that same person asked: "Please don't be offended by my question, Rabbi, but why were you saying those things to yourself?"

"It's like this," Reb Shmelke answered. "I see that the crowd came to honor me, so I was afraid that I might be tempted into arrogance. So first I rehearsed it on my own. It sounded like mockery. That's the sound I'll keep in my ears when others honor me."

104

When Reb Pinches, the author of the *Haflo'oh*, came to Frankfurt to be the rabbi, the entire town came out to welcome him, a whole sea of people.

Later he was asked, "Rabbi, what were you thinking at that moment?"

"I imagined," answered Reb Pinches, "that I was being carried out on my burial boards, and the big crowd was on the way to my funeral."

107

There was a rabbi in Vilna named Reb Moyshe Kremer, who was in fact a *kremer*, a storekeeper. His wife minded the store while he studied day and night.

When he was named the city rabbi, he only accepted the position on condition that he would receive no salary. He would continue supporting himself with the store.

A short time after his appointment, he noticed that his wife had started spending more on the household. He asked her where the extra money came from—did she have a source of income he didn't know about? She explained that now he was the city rabbi, the shop drew customers from all over the city.

Reb Moyshe took out a sheet of paper and calculated how much he needed each week. He instructed his wife: "When you see that you've earned enough for our needs, even if it's Sunday afternoon, I want you to close the shop for the rest of the week. Other Jewish storekeepers need to live, too."

108

Reb Akiva Eiger bitterly disliked his rabbinical duties. In his old age, he tried to get rid of them altogether.

He once heard that the bathhouse keeper in his daughter's town near Posen had died. So he wrote to his daughter and told her he wanted to go manage the bath house. At least in his old age, he explained, he might finally make an honest living.

112

When Reb Elye Ragoler, a disciple of Reb Chaim Volozhiner, received his ordination and accepted a rabbinical post, he went to visit Reb Chaim to take his leave and receive guidance.

Reb Chaim discussed matters of Torah as well as worldly issues with him, instructed him how a rabbi ought to conduct himself, and gave him his blessing.

On the way out, Reb Chaim handed him a small booklet and said, "You should take a look at this. It's something a rabbi absolutely has to know."

Reb Elye was curious to know what Reb Chaim had given him. When he got outside, he opened the booklet: It was a calendar—an ordinary calendar. He was puzzled. Nevertheless, he did what Reb Chaim had told him to do and read the calendar from beginning to end.

He arrived at his new town just before the Sabbath on which the blessings for the New Moon are recited. When he entered the study house, a simple Jew approached him and asked: "Rebbe, at what time will the New Moon appear?"

114

When Reb Yankele Orenstein—the Rabbi of Lemberg and a fierce opponent of modernization—died, the Maskilim of Lemberg refused to let another old-fashioned rabbi be named as his successor. They wanted Lemberg to hire a rabbi who could preach in German, as was fashionable in those days. They built a new synagogue, a "temple," and brought in Reb Avrom Cohen as its rabbi and preacher. They also persuaded the government authorities to name Reb Avrom Cohen as the official rabbi of Lemberg. A fiery dispute broke out in town. People were outraged that a modern German-style rabbi could be the Rabbi of Lemberg. The Hasidim were the most outraged. They considered it outright apostasy.

There was a band of zealots who decided that they needed to get rid of the rabbi. They met, appointed a rabbinical court of twenty-three, a "lesser Sanhedrin," and passed sentence on the rabbi. They ruled that he was guilty of incitement to apostasy and that he should be put to death.

The sentence was immediately carried out. They found a low-down fellow, a certain coppersmith who employed toxic substances for his work. He stole into the rabbi's kitchen and poisoned the food. Reb Avrom Cohen, his wife, and everyone in his household died slow and painful deaths. Only one child survived, but for the rest of his life he remained an invalid.

Naturally, the murder caused quite a sensation in Lemberg. The police were immediately informed, and Jews themselves helped in the investigation.

Before Reb Avrom Cohen died, while his mind was still clear, the investigating magistrate came to interview him. He asked whether he knew or could guess who had done it.

"I don't know," answered Reb Avrom.

"But," the magistrate further probed, "at least we can say, it must have been a Jew?"

"Anyone who would do such a thing," answered Reb Avrom, "is no Jew."

Reb Avrom Cohen was buried as a holy martyr, between the graves of the Taz and the Yeshuos Yankev, Reb Yankele Orenstein. But the zealots stole the corpse from the grave and carried it away—no one knows where.

115

Reb Hirshl Salanter was a world-class scholar, but he remained in Salant all his life and refused to accept a rabbinical post elsewhere, even though several large cities had offered theirs to him.

He wouldn't consider it. Old-time rabbis!

The leading figures of the community of Minsk once came to offer him an appointment. As usual, Reb Hirshl didn't want to accept it. The delegates from Minsk insisted, arguing that Minsk must have the honor of having him as their rabbi and that they had been expressly instructed not to return without his agreement. Reb Hirshl sent them to the rebbetzin—let her agree to it first.

So the delegates went to see the rebbetzin. They showed her the generous salary mentioned in the letter of appointment, and she immediately agreed.

Delighted, they went back to Reb Hirshl, saying, "Your rebbetzin has agreed. Now, rabbi, you must agree too!"

"Let me tell you how it is," responded Reb Hirshl. "My wife, may she live and be well, will be just as good a rebbetzin in Minsk as she is in Salant. But I can barely suffice as a rabbi in Salant—what business do I have being the rabbi in such a great city as Minsk?"

118

Reb Daniel, the *Khamudos Daniel*, was a rabbinical judge in Grodno. They paid him four gulden a week—poverty wages. He subsisted all week on black bread, barley soup, and nothing else.

Once, while he was eating the soup, he realized that it was flavored with chicken fat.

"What happened?" he asked his wife. "How did you get chicken fat?"

She replied, "Our neighbor rendered it today, and she gave me a bit."

When Reb Daniel heard this, he pushed the dish away, recited the prayer after eating, and told the secretary to call a meeting of the trustees.

The trustees came quickly. If Reb Daniel summoned them, it must be something really important, a problem for the whole community!

When they had all assembled, Reb Daniel stood up and said,

"Gentlemen, you should know that today my wife took a bribe from a litigant's wife, and I must resign my position as judge."

120

As a young man, Reb Leybele Kovner refused to accept a rabbinical appointment. He already had a reputation as a great scholar, and several communities had offered him a position. But Reb Leybele preferred to sit and learn Torah for its own sake. Only in middle age did he become a practicing rabbi.

Once he was asked, "Rebbe, why did you wait so long to accept a position?"

"Let me tell you a story," answered Reb Leybele.

> In a certain village there was a peasant, a big drunk. He used to get completely soused and wallow in piles of garbage. So the local landowners' children decided to play a trick on him.
>
> Once, when he was lying there dead drunk, the nobleman's children dressed him up as a priest. They left him there and went off on their way.
>
> The peasant eventually sobered up and rubbed his eyes: Could it be real? Why was he dressed up as a priest? Perhaps he actually was a priest? He touched the clothes: the long black robe, the tall hat—they were all real. And it seemed he was no longer drunk. So he must be a priest!
>
> He thought to himself, "Well, let's check to see if there's a priest-like kind of book in the pocket."
>
> He stuck his hand into the pocket, and indeed it contained the kind of book a priest would carry. More proof that he really was a priest.
>
> Then he reconsidered: "No, I have to see whether I can actually read it."

He opened the book and couldn't read a single letter. Must not be a priest after all.

Then he thought once more, "Well, let's see if the priest himself can read it."

He hauled himself up, went and found the priest, and asked him to read the book. And would you know it—the priest couldn't read it either.

"If that's the case," said the peasant, "then I'm a priest, too."

"It's the same thing with me," concluded Reb Leybele. "At first, I thought that in order to be a rabbi, you had to truly master the Talmud and codes, that you had to spend time with the responsa literature and pietistic tracts. How could I be fit to serve as a rabbi? So I sat and studied. Only later did I find out that rabbis aren't so learned, either. So I could be one, too."

121

When Reb Leybele Kovner was the rabbi of Smorgon, the richest man in town was Reb Dovidl Arendar. Dovidl was a hard man who kept the whole town under his thumb.

One time, Dovidl was party to a lawsuit that came before Reb Leybele. The dispute concerned a large sum of money, and Dovidl was on the verge of losing. The rebbetzin and other members of Reb Leybele's household, knowing who they were dealing with, suggested to Reb Leybele that he shouldn't issue his ruling right away. They urged him not to tell Dovidl that he had lost, but to find some way to appease him, because Dovidl was capable of making Reb Leybele's life pure misery.

"I'll tell you," answered Reb Leybele. "The Torah tells us: *Lo sagoru mipney ish*—'you shall not fear a man.' Now you tell me: which man is it, that we're told not to fear? Moyshe-Dovidl the teacher, who wouldn't hurt a flea? No! It has to mean someone you've got real reason to fear. Someone like Dovidl, for example—now that's the kind of person we're not allowed to be afraid of."

And with that, he ordered the disputants to be brought in and said to the magnate, "Dovidl, you lost the dispute."

As a result, Dovidl became the rabbi's bitter enemy and persecuted him until Reb Leybele was hired away to Kalvarye.

126

In Trestene, a town near Bialystok, there was a rabbi by the name of Reb Shmuel Maggid. His salary was a scant four Polish gulden a week. To earn that pittance, he also had to serve as the custodian, sweeping the study house and keeping the furnace hot in the winter. He made his real living as a blacksmith to support his family. His smithy was right next to the rabbi's house, and there he would shoe horses, repair wagons, and sharpen scythes for the Gentiles.

When he didn't have any jobs to work on in the smithy, he would sit in his house in his tallis and tefillin, studying and issuing decisions on various questions that the Jews of Trestene would bring to him.

If a Gentile needed a horseshoe or a wheel, he would come knock on the window, "Hey, Ravin!"

At that, the rabbi would take off his tallis and tefillin, strap on his toolbelt, and head into the smithy.

And then, if someone came to ask for the rabbi, his wife would answer, "Wait a bit. The rabbi will come soon. He's in the smithy."

127

Reb Nochemke of Grodno was the custodian of the Talmud Society study house. He was desperately poor. Several cities offered Reb Nochemke positions as their rabbi, but he didn't want to take them.

His wife pleaded with him, "Nochem, how long do we have to live like this? Why won't you accept a position, and we'll have a respectable income?"

"Look," said Reb Nochemke. "Here in Grodno, everybody knows

that I'm a simple Jew, a custodian, and they don't bother me. But if I come to a new city, and on top of that I become their rabbi, they'll start testing me and asking me tough questions. When they realize that I'm really an ignoramus, they'll kick me out—and I'll have lost my job as the custodian to boot."

128

Reb Yankev Tsvi Meklenburg, the rabbi of Königsberg, refused to perform any wedding when he couldn't be sure that the ceremony would be carried out properly according to Jewish law.

Once a rich Königsberg resident who was not an observant Jew married off his daughter, and Reb Yankev Tsvi refused to perform the wedding. But the rich man was well-connected. He contacted the government authorities and got them to order the rabbi to perform the wedding, so Reb Yankev Tsvi complied.

When it came to the point where the groom declares that he is betrothed to the bride, Reb Yankev Tsvi began in the usual fashion, prompting the groom word by word: "*Harey* (behold) *at* (you) *mekudeshes* (are betrothed) *li* (to me)." But he changed the last words from "*ke-das* (according to the law of) *Moyshe ve-Yisroel* (Moses and Israel)" to "*ke-das* (according to the law of) Frederick the Great."

"Frederick the Great?! '*Ke-das Moyshe ve-Yisroel*,'" everyone corrected him.

"No," said Reb Yankev Tsvi, "this wedding isn't according to the law of Moses and Israel. But I do have to obey the government."

134

Reb Yosele Slonimer, Reb Ayzl Slonimer's son-in-law, detested the rabbinate. When he was ready to marry off his daughter, he said, "I'm looking for a son-in-law who's a complete ignoramus, through and through. These days, even if he only knew Hebrew and nothing else, I couldn't be sure they wouldn't go and make him a rabbi."

136

Reb Yoshe Ber was sitting with the wealthy men of Brisk, arguing about a certain issue. The rich men, as you would expect, were stubborn as oxen and refused to concede to the rabbi. Meanwhile, Reb Yoshe Ber noticed a woman standing and waiting by the door. He invited her in.

"Rebbe," the woman said, "I've come to ask you to interpret a dream for me. Last night I dreamed that my one and only son had, God forbid, gone crazy."

"An excellent dream," smiled Reb Yoshe Ber. "It's a sign that first of all, God willing, your son will grow up to be wealthy. After all, rich men are all crazy. And you, for your part," he added, turning to the rich men, "think that all rabbis are crazy. So no doubt you'll add that her son will become a rabbi, too."

137

The small town of Korelitz always had the finest rabbis, who would go on to become famous and then get hired away by larger cities.

One time Korelitz was searching for a rabbi. As always, they wanted someone who was outstanding in every respect: a great scholar and an imposing presence. They asked Reb Yoshe Ber of Brisk whether he had anyone to recommend. Reb Yoshe Ber answered that he had a fine rabbi in mind, someone currently living in Brisk. The community sent two respected members to Brisk with a letter of appointment in hand.

As soon as they arrived in Brisk, they went to see Reb Yoshe Ber. When they entered his courtroom, the only person there was a young man, thin and slight with a scraggly beard, standing next to the bookcase and looking into one book after another.

"Where's the rabbi?" they asked.

"He'll come in soon," he replied, his nose in a book.

They sat down to wait. Meanwhile, they noticed that the young man's clothes were old and torn. His coat was in patches and his shoes misshapen from wear. His hair poked through the crown of his hat. They figured he was a poor solitary scholar who had come to see the rabbi.

Reb Yoshe Ber arrived, greeted them, and asked where they were from.

"From Korelitz," they answered.

"Ah, from Korelitz? You came to pick up the rabbi I recommended to you? There he is—come over here, Reb Elye Boruch," he called out to the young man.

The two messengers were astonished. This skinny fellow in his torn clothes was going to be their rabbi?

Some time later, after they'd chatted for a while and Reb Elye Boruch had stepped out, one of the two delegates screwed up his courage and said to Reb Yoshe Ber, "Please don't be offended, Rebbe. If you tell us we should hire him as our rabbi, obviously he must be qualified. But Rebbe, you know that our town is used to having good-looking rabbis with a commanding presence, and this young man is somehow—"

Before he could finish Reb Yoshe Ber shouted to his secretary, "Yankl, come here!"

The secretary came in.

"Take these two Jews over to the slaughterhouse, and show them Berl the butcher."

The two men stared at Reb Yoshe Ber.

Angrily, Reb Yoshe Ber explained, "You're obviously looking for a rabbi who's a healthy young man, tall and broad shouldered. So go with my secretary. He'll show you whom to pick."

The Korelitz Jews were mortified, and they began to excuse themselves: "Rebbe, please don't be offended, we didn't mean..."

"All right, so take the rabbi I'm giving you," smiled Reb Yoshe Ber, "and go home in joy and peace."

Reb Eliyahu Boruch accepted the appointment, and served as the rabbi of Korelitz until he was hired by Mir.

138

Once during Reb Yoshe Ber's tenure as rabbi of Slutsk, the local official who supervised collection of the tax on kosher slaughter came to him, shouting, "Rabbi, they're bringing in meat that was slaughtered outside of town!"

"All right, so what's the big deal?" asked Reb Yoshe Ber.

"What?!'" replied the official in astonishment. "Outside slaughterers, how can we trust that their meat is kosher?"

"Don't worry about it," smiled Reb Yoshe Ber. "It's a simple matter of logic. Since Slutsk's slaughterers—whose practices we know all too well—are nonetheless still acceptable to us, all the more so should we accept slaughterers whom we don't know at all."

139

The same official, Avreml Yavrov, once gave a milk cow to Reb Yoshe Ber as a present.

A few weeks later, Yavrov came to Reb Yoshe Ber and asked him to forbid the consumption of meat slaughtered out of town. Not only did Reb Yoshe Ber refuse to do this, but right then and there he called in his wife and said, "Give Avreml back his cow right now, and pay him for the milk, too."

140

When Reb Yoshe Ber left Slutsk, he spent some time without a rabbinical position and without any income.

Once while riding the train, he met a Jew from Brisk, one of its leading citizens. Just then Brisk happened to be looking for a new rabbi. The Jew from Brisk began discussing the position with Reb Yoshe Ber.

"Take my advice," said Reb Yoshe Ber, "and hire Reb Yehoshua Leyb Diskin. He'll do an excellent job."

Only several years later, after Reb Yehoshua Leyb left Brisk, did Reb Yoshe Ber come to serve as the rabbi there.

141

Reb Yoshe Ber had a saying:

"There are two people in this world who don't know the measure of their own strength: the town constable and—*lehavdil*—the town rabbi.

"The first—the town constable—is like an emperor. He can do whatever he wants: issue decrees, impose punishments, put people in prison—who dares oppose him? Nevertheless he's but a simple Gentile and whiles away his time drinking with the peasants in the tavern.

"The second—the rabbi—rules his own kingdom. He answers questions about Jewish law, declares food kosher and nonkosher, issues summons, declares this one's claim valid and that one's claim invalid, prohibits, imposes fines—and yet it never occurs to him to ask: What is the basis of his power, really? What would he do if people didn't obey?"

146

Reb Meir Simche was the rabbi of Dvinsk for 39 years. During the Great War, when Dvinsk was right in the line of fire, everyone fled from the city. Whoever could escape, did. Only the city's paupers, those without any resources or help, remained.

Reb Meir Simche was urged to flee, since it was getting more dangerous every day.

"No," answered Reb Meir Simche, "as long as there are nine Jews left in Dvinsk, I'll be the tenth."

148

A rabbi once had a dispute with the people of his town. Reb Yitschok Yankev Reines was brought in to rule on the dispute. He ruled that the townspeople should pay the rabbi a settlement and that the rabbi should resign.

The bargaining began. The town wanted to pay a hundred rubles, but the rabbi insisted on no less than three hundred.

"The rabbi is right," Reb Yitschok Yankev said to the leaders of the community. "Give him three hundred rubles."

"What?" argued the community leaders. "Why should he get three hundred rubles? A hundred isn't enough?"

"Let me explain," said Reb Yitschok Yankev with a smile. "You're ready to pay him to leave. If anyone knows exactly how much it's worth to get rid of him, it's the man himself."

149

A certain rabbi complained to Reb Yitschok Yankev Reines that he was being persecuted by Hasidim who suspected him of being a Maskil, more concerned with grammar and propriety than traditional Jewish practice.

"I have some advice for you," Reb Yitschok Yankev said to him.

"What is it?" the rabbi eagerly replied.

"Try writing them a letter," said Reb Yitschok Yankev, "and immediately they'll see that their suspicion is completely unfounded."

150

Reb Moyshe Itsl, the rabbi of Ponevezh, was more of a merchant than a rabbi. He dealt in various goods: Prussian tea, Prussian cigars, textiles, and even horses. His business frequently took him out of town.

He used to joke, "Ponevezh would have come and fired me a long time ago—if they could ever find me."

152

Reb Elye Chaim of Lodz was extremely generous and always gave more charity than he could afford. His salary didn't suffice, and he was always in debt.

During his many years in Lodz, the Jewish community of Warsaw offered him a contract to serve as their rabbi several times, since he was one of the outstanding leaders of his generation. Reb Elye Chaim refused every time.

"Rebbe," he was once asked, "why don't you take the position? Such a prominent community like Warsaw!"

"Here's how it is," answered Reb Elye Chaim. "As you know, I spend more than I earn, and I'm always racking up debts. Now, why does anybody still loan to me? Against my wealth? Against some property of mine? No, the only reason why they lend me money is that they think one day a larger community will come and hire me, and they'll pay off my debts as part of the package. And that's how it's always been. When I was the rabbi of Dretshin, I borrowed money against the post in Pruzhene. When I was in Pruzhene, I borrowed money against the post in Lodz. Now that I'm here, I borrow against Warsaw—but if I go off to Warsaw, against what will I borrow?"

156

Reb Yechezkl Landau, the author of *Noda B'Yehuda*, was once approached by two rich men of Prague who had an odd dispute.

They were neighbors who lived in the same house. A street musician had stood at their door and played beautifully. They fell into arguing over which one of them the musician had serenaded. Each claimed that the musician had played for him. So they came to Reb Yechezkl, and right then and there placed on the table forty gulden as their fee for his ruling.

Reb Yechezkl heard out both sides and said to the rich men with a smile, "The musician played neither for you, nor for you—he played for me, so that I could get forty gulden."

157

Someone came to Reb Yechezkl Landau, the *Noda B'Yehuda*, and complained, "What should I do, Rebbe? I can't find time to pick up a book. People keep distracting me. They won't leave me alone for a minute."

"Here's my advice," answered Reb Yechezkl. "Rich people are coming to you? Ask them for a free loan, and you'll never see them again. Poor people? *Give* them a free loan, and you'll never see them, either."

158

[Regionally famous tsaddikim (considered wonderworkers) could overshadow local rabbinic authorities if they were not careful.]

When Reb Shmelke of Nikolsburg was passing through Krakow, a mother brought her child to him, weeping: "Holy Rebbe, save us! My little child—the only one I have left—is very sick."

The visiting tzaddik took a kerchief, wrapped something up in it, handed it to the woman, and said, "Give it to the town rabbi and he'll tell you what to do."

She went to see the rabbi, Reb Yitschok Landau, uncle to the *Noda B'Yehuda*, and gave him the kerchief. Reb Yitschok unwrapped it and found a golden coin. He was puzzled. Then he remembered that there was a famous doctor in town just then who charged exactly that amount per visit. He said to the woman, "Take the coin and go see the doctor."

161

A servant girl once came to Reb Abele Posvoler, the Rabbi of Vilna, with the following question: "Rebbe, what should I make for lunch?"

"Go home," said the rabbi, "and make noodles."

Those present were surprised at this strange question and answer.

"What don't you understand?" Reb Abele said to them. "The girl asks the lady of the house, 'What should I make for lunch?' The lady shoots back, 'What should you make? Go ask the Rabbi!' The girl took it literally, and came to ask me."

162

Reb Abele Posvoler, the Rabbi of Vilna, would write letters of reference on behalf of people who had failed in business or whose homes had burned down and had taken to the roads as beggars. He was good-natured and couldn't turn anyone down, so whoever came and asked for such a letter got one.

Once, a Jew came to him claiming that he had two daughters to marry off and no money. Would the rabbi write a letter attesting that this man was entitled to alms to cover his wedding expenses?

A few days later, the man was found passed out in the street, dead drunk, with Reb Abele's letter lying on the ground next to him. They took the letter to Reb Abele: "You see who you're writing letters for, Rebbe?"

When the man sobered up, he came back to Reb Abele with some kind of sob story. He had lost the letter and needed the rabbi to write him another.

"You know," responded Reb Abele, "there's a common saying, 'drunk as Lot.' Now this raises a question: Why Lot, rather than Noah? Noah got drunk too, and he lived long before Lot. The answer is: Noah got drunk after he had already married off all his children. Not so bad. But Lot still had two daughters to marry off. A father in that situation must not get drunk."

164

A scribe once came to show Reb Hirsh Melech Dinever a sheet from a Torah scroll he had just written.

Reb Hirsh Melech gazed at the sheet in silence.

"How do you like the calligraphy, Rebbe?" asked the scribe.

"The calligraphy is calligraphy," answered Reb Hirsh Melech, "but the words are simply out of this world."

166

A good number of Jews in Lemberg used to sneak into a certain Gentile-owned restaurant in the city to enjoy a nonkosher meal.

Eventually, the woman who ran the restaurant came to the rabbi, Reb Yankele Orenstein, complaining that Jews would come in, run up big bills, and never pay up.

"Here's my advice," said Reb Yankele. "The first Jew that comes in tomorrow, give him one big bill covering everything all the other Jews owe you. If he doesn't want to pay it, summon him to the rabbi."

The next day, a Jew came into the restaurant, sat himself down, and ordered a lavish meal. After he ate, the owner gave him a bill that made him nearly faint.

"What?" he protested. "How could one meal cost that much?"

"That's what all your brother Jews who eat here owe me."

"Why should I have to pay for all the other Jews?" he argued.

"Let's go see the rabbi," she responded.

As soon as he heard this, he pulled out his wallet, paid, and disappeared.

The woman went right back to the rabbi and thanked him for his advice.

167

There once was a bitter dispute in Berdichev concerning a kosher slaughterer. The town had an elderly slaughterer named Avrom, an expert in the controversial procedure of removing deposits on the lungs of animals in order to render the rest of the animal kosher. Certain parties in town began spreading rumors that he was supplying nonkosher meat. Some supported the slaughterer, and others were against him. Some said his meat was kosher, others said it wasn't. And the town knew no peace.

Eventually it was agreed that the Maggid of Brody, Reb Shloyme Kluger, would be brought in, and that everyone would abide by his ruling.

Reb Shloyme Kluger agreed to come to Berdichev, but on condition that he would only issue his ruling once he returned home, not on the spot.

Reb Shloyme came to Berdichev, questioned the slaughterer, observed how he slaughtered and how he checked the lungs, and prepared to return to Brody. But a certain hitch came up in relation to his travel documents, so he had to stay in Berdichev for another three weeks.

The whole town of Berdichev was eager to know how he had ruled. Every day, Berdichevers came to see Reb Shloyme on various pretexts, trying any way they could think of to get him to reveal his ruling. But each time, Reb Shloyme refused to tell them.

So the richest man in town, Reb Yisroel Halpern, tried to pry it out of him. He said to Reb Shloyme: "Rebbe, everyone in town knows that I can keep a secret. You can entrust your biggest secret to me, and not a soul will find out. So, Rebbe, tell me how you're ruling about that slaughterer."

"What a fine trait that is," smiled Reb Shloyme. "I'm going to learn a lesson from you and keep this a secret."

169

A woman came to Reb Shayele Kutner with a question about a chicken. While she was koshering it, she couldn't find the gallbladder. A chicken missing a gallbladder is not kosher, but if you can detect traces of its bitterness, that's good enough.

Reb Shayele licked the liver, and it wasn't bitter. He gave it to the judges, who also licked it and didn't sense any bitterness. Then he said to the woman, "You try licking it."

The woman licked the liver.

"Is it bitter?" Reb Shayele asked her.

"Oy, my dear Rebbinke!" the woman sighed. "It's bitter as death. I'm a widow with little orphans. My older boy studies well, but he's gotten sick, so the doctor told me to cook him a chicken soup. I saved the last of my money and bought a chicken. And my luck—the chicken might not be kosher. Oy, how bitter it is, Rebbinke!"

"If it's bitter," ruled Reb Shayele, "then it's kosher."

170

Reb Ayzl Slonimer tended to be extremely lenient in his rulings. His rabbinical judge, however, was very stringent.

Once, they were discussing the general issue of leniency and stringency. Reb Ayzl argued, "Look, here's how it is. You don't always have to rule like the law is written. But the law always has to be written like you rule."

171

A widow once came to Reb Yitschok Vurker with a claim against two merchants who had owed money to her late husband. Reb Yitschok ruled that the merchants must pay the woman, but since they were of modest means, they could pay in installments.

When the widow went away, the merchants said to the rabbi, "Rebbe, how can you believe that brazen woman? Her husband has been dead for more than three years, but she had a baby just six months ago!"

"What?" Reb Yitschok responded with a start. "That's the situation? Then pay her the whole thing at once!"

172

When Reb Leybele was rabbi of Kovno, there was a matchmaker named Rifoel. Rifoel was known far and wide as someone who arranged the most prominent matches between the wealthiest and most prominent families.

One time, Rifoel was on the brink of concluding a brilliant match. The dowry was in the thousands, and Rifoel stood to earn a hefty fee. The groom was from Kovno and the bride from a distant city. As usual, Rifoel praised the groom, saying he was the complete package—an accomplished Talmud scholar and well-versed in secular culture as well. Nevertheless, the father of the bride demanded a letter signed by the rabbi of Kovno testifying to the groom's Torah scholarship.

Rifoel got nervous. It wasn't easy to get that kind of letter from Reb Leybele. In order to get him to certify someone as learned, the latter had to be a real genius.

But Rifoel was a master matchmaker, after all. He had an idea. He would get the letter from Reb Leybele's son, Reb Moyshe Shmuel, who was a member of the rabbinical court. That would be enough to satisfy the bride's father. Right away, Rifoel approached Reb Leybele's son, promising to repay him for his trouble, and obtained the letter.

The match went through, and the wedding was held. Rifoel received his fee, and then he went and found Reb Moyshe Shmuel sitting in the courtroom and handed him twenty-five rubles. Reb Moyshe Shmuel said it was not enough and he didn't want to take it. They started negotiating, and meanwhile Reb Leybele walked in. "What are you arguing about?" he asked.

"We've got a bit of a dispute here," said Rifoel. "By all means, Rebbe, why don't you judge it?"

"If you'll accept my ruling," answered Reb Leybele, sitting down at the table, "let's hear your claims."

When Reb Leybele heard what the dispute was about, he sprang up angrily and turned to his son: "Moyshe Shmuel, what did you do? If the groom is really learned, you were obliged to write the letter for free. If not—you're getting paid to write lies. Gentlemen," he said to everyone else in the room, "you should immediately remove my son as a member of the court. He is unfit to judge."

173

The rabbi of Warsaw, Reb Berish Meisels, was once interrupted in his study by a Jew who came in shouting, "Rebbe, save me! I'm ruined!"

"Sit down and tell me what happened," replied Reb Berish.

The man told his story to Reb Berish:

"I'm not from here. I'm a merchant, and I came to Warsaw to do some trading. I arrived on Friday with 5,000 rubles cash, which I had to put away until after Shabbos, and I was afraid to keep it at an inn. So I went to the home of an acquaintance, a well-known merchant in Warsaw. On Friday before candle lighting time, I gave him the 5,000 rubles to hide until after Shabbos. On Sunday morning, I asked him for the money since I needed to go do business. He claimed he had no idea what I was talking about. I nearly fainted: 'What do you mean? On Friday evening I myself handed you the money!' We went back and forth, and he kept insisting that there was no more to say. What can I do, Rebbe? The sky is falling and I don't know where else to turn. I've lost my money."

"Have faith," replied the rabbi. "With God's help, you'll get your money back. I'll summon him to my office. Meanwhile, you go wait out of sight in the next room. When you hear me raise my voice, come in."

The rabbi summoned the Warsaw merchant on the pretext that he had to discuss civic matters with him, and the merchant came right away. The rabbi invited him to sit down and began to chat casually with him in a friendly fashion. Suddenly, he started to speak loudly. At that, the man from out of town came in from the next room, and when he saw the Warsaw merchant, he began to shout, "Rebbe, that's him! He's trying to ruin me. Make him pay me back my money!"

"Do you know this man?" the rabbi asked the Warsaw merchant.

"Yes, Rebbe," he calmly replied. "I know him. He stayed with me for Shabbos. He ate and drank at my table. And now he's claiming that I stole 5,000 rubles from him. Clearly, this man is out of his mind."

The man from out of town glared daggers at him. "You personally took the money from my hand on Friday before candle-lighting, and you counted it all out before my very eyes. How could a Jew have the heart to do such an abominable thing?"

"You see," said the rabbi to the Warsaw merchant, "you're not going to get rid of this man so easily. Give him a few rubles and that'll take care of it."

"If that's what you're telling me to do, Rebbe," said the Warsaw merchant, "then I'll obey. I'm willing to give him 25 rubles if he'll just leave me alone."

But the out-of-towner wouldn't hear of it. "What's he giving me? A piece of rope to hang myself!"

"Give him a few more rubles," said the rabbi.

"I obey your word, Rebbe," repeated the Warsaw merchant. "I'll give him 50 rubles, and let that be the end of it."

But the out-of-towner didn't stop crying and shouting, and declared that if the Warsaw merchant didn't give him back his 5,000 rubles, he'd kill him with his bare hands!

"You see that it's going to take more to extricate yourself," said the rabbi to the Warsaw merchant. "Take my advice and give him 100 rubles."

"I'll do it for your sake, Rebbe," said the Warsaw merchant. "I'll give that bum 100 rubles to make him go away."

But the out-of-towner still wouldn't hear of it.

"What do you want?" thundered the rabbi, pretending to be angry at the out-of-towner. "A hundred rubles is generous."

"I don't want generosity," wept the out-of-towner. "I want my money."

"You know what?" the rabbi said to the Warsaw merchant. "Try one more time. Give him 500 rubles."

"If you tell me to do it, Rebbe, I'll do it."

At that, the rabbi stood up and shouted at the Warsaw merchant: "You lowlife! You good-for-nothing! Pay this man back his 5,000 rubles! Now I'm sure you took it from him. I know how stingy you are. I recently asked you for a measly 10 rubles for charity and you refused. And now you're ready to hand over 500 rubles just like that? You're not leaving here. I'm letting the police know about this, and we'll find those 5,000 rubles at your house."

When the Warsaw merchant heard this, his face grew white as chalk, and he confessed to the whole thing. The out-of-towner got his 5,000 rubles back.

174

Reb Moyshe Savraner was famous for being a Hasidic rebbe who was also quite worldly.

Once when he was in Berdichev, a Jew who had the air of a great merchant approached him and confided in him as follows:

"I'm from Brody," he began. "My name is Dovid Poyzner. I'm a broker. Praise God, I do big deals, especially in Russia. One of the merchants I deal with, a rich man from Balta, owed me a thousand rubles. As is the normal practice, he gave me a promissory note for that amount. After a while, the time came for me to send him a list of the goods he owed me as compensation. I wrote out the list and placed it in a small chest where I had the Balta merchant's accounts and his note. That's how I do it—I keep each merchant's accounts in a separate compartment. On the day that the mail was supposed to be picked up, I told my daughter, who helps out with the business, to send out the list of goods to the Balta merchant, along with a cover letter. The next day, I go to the compartment: the list is still there. This puzzles me. I ask my daughter whether she's mailed it off. She says, 'Yes,' so I showed it to her.

"Then we looked around and realized that the promissory note is missing. My daughter made a mistake and sent him the promissory note instead of the list. A thousand rubles on the line! So I sent him the list with a letter explaining the mistake and requesting him to send the note back. Some time passed with no answer. I wrote to him again, and a third time—he answered that he hasn't the foggiest idea what I'm talking about. He never gave me any note. In short, Rebbe, what should I do? Give me some advice. Tell me how I can get my money back."

Reb Moyshe heard him out and said, "In three weeks, you should come to Balta. I'll be there. And God will help."

Three weeks later, the Brody merchant came to Balta and went straightaway to Reb Moyshe to ask what he should do next.

"Summon that Balta merchant to appear before me for a trial," said Reb Moyshe. "I'll hear both sides and issue a ruling."

Both merchants appeared before Reb Moyshe for the ruling. The curious case also drew a large audience. The Brody merchant claimed that he had been holding the Balta merchant's note for 1,000 rubles and had sent it off to him by mistake. The Balta merchant insisted it never happened: So what else was there to say?

Reb Moyshe listened to both parties and ordered them both to leave. When they were outside, he said to the crowd still in the room, "No one dare leave here until the hearing is over. Later, I'll explain why."

He summoned the parties back in.

When they returned, he said to the Balta merchant: "My ruling is that you are to return the 1,000 rubles to this man."

"What do you mean?" the Balta merchant angrily responded. "How can I return what I never owed? Is 1,000 rubles no big deal to you, Rebbe? And moreover, it will ruin my reputation. People will think I really tried to cheat him—that he really had my note, and I tried to deny it. They'll say I'm a swindler. No, Rebbe, I wouldn't do that kind of thing."

"Are you testing my Divine Sight? Do you want a demonstration?" Reb Moyshe's voice was stern and menacing. "Here you go: On a Friday night, you burned that note in the flames of the very candles that your wife had blessed in honor of the Sabbath!"

When the Balta merchant heard that, he fainted dead away.

When they managed to revive him, Reb Moyshe said to him: "You see, I've just shown you that there is a God in the world who sees everything and does not abandon the just. Send someone right away to tell your wife to bring 1,000 rubles here and give this man back what you stole. Do that, and I'll pray that God shall forgive you."

The Balta merchant did what he had been told.

Then Reb Moyshe turned to the crowd and said: "I told all of you to wait until the end, because I knew that when you left here, each of you would want to relate the miracle of how an angel came down from Heaven and revealed the truth to the Rebbe. I kept you here so that I could show you the angel, so you could see him with your own eyes."

As the people in the crowd began to look around, Reb Moyshe went and opened a door to a side room, from which he led out a boy about thirteen years old. "Look, here's the angel who revealed the truth to me."

The Balta merchant stood there, utterly crushed. The boy was a nephew of his who was being raised in his house.

"Don't touch a hair on this boy's head," Reb Moyshe warned the Balta merchant. "Raise him like your own child, and God will surely forgive you."

Here's how Reb Moyshe found out the truth:

When Reb Moyshe arrived in Balta, he began inquiring about the Balta merchant. He queried everyone who came to see him: Do you know this merchant? How does he deal with God and man? Everyone said that as far as they knew, he was an honest merchant and an upstanding Jew.

Reb Moyshe was close to giving up on the whole affair, until a certain Hebrew teacher came to visit him. Reb Moyshe asked whether he knew the merchant. It turned out that the teacher knew him very well. A nephew of the merchant's, an orphan, was the teacher's student.

"Is he an honest man?" Reb Moyshe asked.

"Yes, it seems so," answered the teacher. "Well, one time the boy mentioned in school that he'd seen his uncle breaking Shabbos. But I know it's impossible. Probably the boy saw something innocent and misinterpreted it. I scolded him, and he hasn't mentioned it since."

Reb Moyshe took careful note. He asked the teacher to bring the boy in without telling anyone else about it.

The teacher brought the boy. Reb Moyshe locked the door, called the boy over, and said, "Don't be afraid, my child. Nothing's going to happen to you. Just tell me the truth. Your teacher told me that you saw your uncle violating Shabbos. Tell me what you saw."

The terrified boy told Reb Moyshe, "One Friday night, when I got back home from shul with my uncle and we began to sing 'Sholem-aleykhem,' the postman brought in a sealed letter. My uncle told me to open the envelope, and he took out a letter and a small slip of paper. When he saw the paper, he jumped up and began to read the letter. Everyone in the house realized it would be a while before my uncle said Kiddush, so they went to their rooms. But I hid behind the wall hangings. I saw my uncle look around, grab the piece of paper and burn it in the flame of the Shabbos candles."

Reb Moyshe immediately understood that the letter that had been sent from Brody was delivered in Balta on Friday night, and that the piece of paper was the promissory note.

"Go home, my child," Reb Moyshe told the boy. "Don't be afraid. Soon I'll summon you."

175

Reb Moyshe Savraner once spent time in a certain town where, as it turned out, his powers of perception were badly needed.

A local wine merchant had just hired a new servant who—over the years of his service elsewhere—had sweated and saved a penny here and a nickel there, until he'd assembled fifty rubles. He always kept the money on his person, except of course on Shabbos. That Friday before candle-lighting time, the servant went down into the cellar and hid his money among the wine barrels.

On Saturday evening after Havdalah, he went down into the cellar, and the money wasn't there. Since he and the master were the only ones who ever went down into the cellar, he ran back upstairs to the master, weeping and demanding his money back. The latter just looked at him. What could he possibly have to say? The servant collapsed to the floor. Those few rubles were his entire fortune! The master, however, insisted that he didn't have any idea what had happened. On the contrary, he was insulted and angry that the servant was falsely accusing him!

The servant saw that he wasn't getting anywhere, so he went to see Reb Moyshe Savraner. He fell at Reb Moyshe's feet and begged him to help get the money back. Reb Moyshe heard the whole story and summoned the wine merchant. The latter stuck to his story:

What could he possibly have to say?

"Did you steal the money?" Reb Moyshe asked him again.

"No!"

"If so," Reb Moyshe said, "it could well be that a non-Jew was rooting around the cellar and found the money. Who knows, he could have touched any or all of your wine casks, and now we can't trust that they're still kosher. If it was touched by a non-Jew, I'll have to declare all of your wine forbidden."

When the wine merchant heard this, he was terrified. He realized that he risked losing thousands of rubles' worth of wine.

"Rebbe," he began to stammer, overcome with humiliation, "I... I took the money."

"How can I be sure," Reb Moyshe insisted, unrelenting, "that you took the money, rather than some Gentile?"

"Rebbe," the wine merchant swore, "may terrible calamities befall me if I'm lying! With my own two hands I took the money from among the barrels."

He continued to passionately swear, with great pain and evident sorrow, until he finally managed to convince Reb Moyshe that he himself had indeed stolen the servant's money.

178

Two men once came to Reb Lipele Bialystoker, the author of *Oyneg Yom Tov*, to ask him to adjudicate a dispute concerning a piece of undeveloped real estate. Both of them were stubborn, and Reb Lipele couldn't get them to compromise. So he went with them to go take a look at the disputed lot.

When they arrived, the litigants volunteered their complaints and started quarreling all over again. Reb Lipele bent over his body with his ear toward the ground and remained that way for some time.

"What are you doing, Rebbe?" wondered the disputants.

"It's like this," answered Reb Lipele. "You're arguing about this piece of earth. One of you says, 'It's mine,' and the other, 'No, it's mine!' So I figured, let's hear what the earth has to say for itself. And it's this: 'Sooner or later, both of you will be mine...'"

180

Reb Shmuel Salant didn't believe in Hasidic miracle-working. He didn't grant blessings, hand out amulets, or recommend supernatural remedies.

One evening, a man whose wife was experiencing a difficult labor came to seek his help. The situation was growing desperate. She had already been in labor since early in the morning.

"What have you tried?" asked Reb Shmuel.

"The doctor's come three times already," he answered. "We did what he told us to, but it hasn't helped."

"Go home," said Reb Shmuel. "Within half an hour, all will be well."

Three quarters of an hour later, the man's neighbors ran to Reb Shmuel and said, "Mazel tov, Rebbe! Your blessing was precisely fulfilled. Thirty minutes after you spoke, the woman gave birth."

Reb Shmuel's guests gazed at each other in wonder.

"Don't go thinking this was some kind of miracle!" said Reb Shmuel. "Every one of you could have done the same thing. It's quite simple. The woman had been in labor for twelve hours; the doctor had already come and given her the necessary medicines and treatments. How much longer could it possibly take? Another half hour at most."

182

Reb Sholem Ber Kletsker was extraordinarily lenient. The town's rabbinical judge, however, was stringent.

A difficult question once arose. Reb Sholem Ber sat with the dayan, looking at sources, thinking it over, and coming up with arguments that the item was kosher. The dayan refused to agree. He cited the clear, stringent ruling of one of the later authorities. Reb Sholem Ber continued arguing with him, bringing several more points in favor of a ruling of "kosher." But the dayan insisted: Here it is written explicitly that we must rule stringently.

"Let me tell you a story," Reb Sholem Ber said.

Once, there was an informer in a certain town. He created terrible problems, helping the "local authorities" put pressure on his fellow Jews. The community thought they might get rid of him by getting him drafted, so in their next report to the draft committee, they wrote down that he was only 21 years old.

The draft committee came and ordered the informer to report. He rushed in and started to argue: "What are you talking about, how could I be drafted, I'm way over age, I'm over 40!"

"In our records," they answered, "you're recorded as being 21."

He argued further: "How could I be 21, if I already have a 25-year-old son?" He ran off and brought back his son, who was himself already a grown man with his own wife and children.

But the officials stuck to their guns: "A son? His own wife and kids? So what? Right here it clearly says you're 21 years old!"

And he was drafted into the army.

183

Reb Avrom Zhetler was once approached by the town's butchers with a difficult religious question. It was just before Passover. The townspeople needed meat, but the butchers were terribly poor, so they had borrowed the money to buy the ox, which—once butchered—revealed itself to have some concerning flaws. Reb Avrom wanted to declare the ox kosher, but according to the standards of the preeminent authority, Reb Moyshe Isserles, known as the Remo, it simply wasn't kosher. He searched in all his books until he found one rabbi who in a similar case had ruled leniently. He said to the town's religious judge, "Let's take the responsibility of declaring it kosher on ourselves—I'll take some, and you take some."

"God forbid!" the judge shrank back. "Go against the Remo?"
And so Reb Avrom himself declared the ox kosher.

"How could you do that?" the judge asked him. "Do you really have the conviction to take on the holy Remo?"

"Here's how I see it," replied Reb Avrom. "If I declared the ox nonkosher, then in the World to Come I would face a complaint from the butchers. They'd drag me before the Heavenly Court and claim that I'd made them utterly destitute. They owed money they could no longer pay back—the best they could do would be to sell the meat to Gentiles at a loss. Now just go try and plead your case with coarse, everyday Jews.

"So I ruled it kosher, and now in Heaven, I'll face a complaint from the Remo. All right—with a scholar and saint like that I can reach some kind of understanding."

184

Reb Meir Michl, the rabbi of Shat, was terribly afraid to issue halakhic rulings, lest his rulings turn out to be incorrect. One time, he was seen chasing after a Jew whose chicken he had just declared nonkosher, begging the man to at least let him pay for the chicken. Eventually he resigned from his post, and he never served as a rabbi thereafter.

186

Reb Moyshe Itsl of Ponevezh once presided over an unusual dispute.

Two Jews had together purchased cemetery plots for themselves, and a dispute arose between them, each one claiming that he had the right to the better of the two gravesites. They argued and argued until they eventually brought the dispute to Reb Moyshe Itsl.

Reb Moyshe Itsl heard each one out and then gave the following decision: "Whoever dies first gets the better grave."

They never uttered a word about it again.

188

Once they asked Reb Chaim Brisker:

"If a known thief invites you to a feast, are you allowed to eat there?"

Reb Chaim told them to wait for his answer, and sent for the Senior Thief of Brisk.

The thief came right away. After all, it was the rabbi calling. Reb Chaim went into a private room with him and said, "Listen, I want to ask you something, but you should answer me honestly. You know that you have nothing to fear from me."

"Yes, Rebbe, ask me," said the thief. "I will tell you the absolute truth."

"Tell me," Reb Chaim asked, "what happens when thieves have an opportunity to steal on Shabbos?"

"We take it," calmly answered the thief.

"What about if you need to light a fire?"

"We light it."

"And what if you need to break a lock?"

"We break it."

"Tell me," Reb Chaim asked further, "what do you think about robbing a Gentile?"

"All right, so he's a Gentile," the thief replied with a smug grin. "Gentile money isn't money?"

"What if the Gentile has a side of treyf meat or a bit of pork?"

"We take it."

"What do you do with it?"

"We sell it to a Gentile."

"Why don't you eat it yourselves?"

"What do you mean?" wondered the thief, astonished. "Eat treyf? Eat pork?"

"Look," Reb Chaim said. "According to you, stealing from others is all right. Lighting fires and breaking locks on Shabbos is all right. So what's different about eating treyf?"

"No offense, Rebbe," the thief replied, offended. "You of all people should say that? Thievery is our livelihood, and if it happens to fall on Shabbos, look, what can you do? But eating treyf? What, aren't we Jews?"

"You can go now, and be well," Reb Chaim said to him.

A while later, Reb Chaim returned to those who were waiting for him and informed them, "You may eat at the thief's feast."

191

There once was a preacher in Tiktin. He approached the rabbi, Reb Meirl, to ask for permission to give a sermon in the synagogue. Reb Meirl gave him permission and then went to hear what he would have to say.

The preacher's sermon was fiery, in the old style. He scolded the congregation for their great sins against each other and against God, and he exhorted them to repent. Throughout the whole speech, Reb Meirl stood, raptly listening to each and every word with tears pouring from his eyes.

After the sermon was complete and the crowd had left, Reb Meirl said to the preacher, "Thank you for the righteous rebuke. But did you have to embarrass me in public? You couldn't have rebuked me in private?"

"Rebbe, what are you talking about?" the preacher trembled in fear. "God forbid—I didn't mean you! I meant the congregation."

"No, no, no," Reb Meirl replied guilelessly, "Jews are all holy. When you talked about errors and misdeeds, you obviously meant the only sinner and evildoer here—me."

192

An itinerant preacher once came to Tiktin to give a fiery Shabbos sermon. He accused the congregation of using false weights and measures.

Reb Meirl, the Rabbi of Tiktin, ascended the podium and said, "Master of the Universe, don't listen to him! There's not one true word in what he says. Jews are extremely careful to use fair weights and measures."

197

The Maggid of Slutsk, *Moyshe Yidaber* (Moyshe Speaks), was a fine-looking man. He had a flowing beard, he always dressed carefully, and he looked like a rabbi.

He once boarded a train and entered a car that was packed full of Jews. There wasn't even standing room. As soon as he came in, people began to murmur, "A rabbi! A rabbi!"

The crowd squeezed together and made way for him to walk through. Then someone got up and offered the Maggid his seat.

"Please sit, Rebbe."

The Maggid sat down.

As Jews do, the other passengers began chatting with him.

"Where are you coming from, Rebbe?"

"And where are you headed?"

"And in which town are you the rabbi?"

"I'm not a rabbi," said Reb Moyshe, "I'm the Maggid of Slutsk."

As soon as he said that, the Jew who had given up his seat said, "Excuse me, sir—that spot is taken."

The poor preacher had to get up, and for the rest of the journey he remained standing on his two feet.

199

Reb Shabsai Cohen, the great scholar known as the Shach, was one of the trustees of the Jewish community of Vilna. The city needed to hire a cantor. The Shach wanted to hire Reb Moyshe Rivkes, author of *Be'er Hagolah*, who was a great scholar and terribly poor, without two pennies to rub together.

"What are you thinking, Rebbe?" the other trustees complained. "Moyshe Rivkes can barely carry a tune."

"According to Jewish law," answered the Shach, "a cantor must have the following virtues: He must be a scholar, God-fearing, possess a distinguished countenance, and finally, be able to sing well. Reb Moyshe Rivkes has the first three qualities, so what if he lacks the last? You tell me, where are you going to find a cantor who possesses every single one of the required virtues?"

200

Slonim was famous for its great cantors, but the cantors never stayed very long. As soon as a cantor in Slonim gained a reputation, a bigger city would come in, offer better pay, and snatch him away.

When Yoshe Slonimer came to take up the position, the townspeople decided to take particular precautions lest he, too, leave quickly. They called a council meeting and decided that the cantor would have to sign a contract promising to stay in Slonim for a certain number of years. The trustees went to the rabbi, Reb Ayzl Kharif, to ask him how best to draw up the contract.

"Let me tell you a story," said Reb Ayzl.

> Once upon a time, a Jewish community made a new cemetery. Nobody wanted to be the first one buried there, as is the superstition. So the burial society announced that not only would the first dead person to consecrate the new graveyard receive their burial for free, but their heirs would be paid 100 gulden, too! Yet more time passed, and the new cemetery still lay unconsecrated. Everyone who died wrote in their will that they should be buried in the old graveyard, not the new one.
>
> There was a fellow in town who was a poor but easygoing type. Passover was approaching, and he didn't have money to buy food for the holiday. His wife began pestering him, "What will we do? Passover's around the corner, but you wouldn't know it from looking at our house."
>
> "I have an idea," he said. "Just do exactly as I say. I'll pretend I've died, and you go to the burial society and tell them that before dying, I'd agreed to

be buried at the new cemetery. You'll get the 100 gulden, and we'll have us a fine Passover."

And that's just what she did. She placed him on the ground on a bed of straw, covered him with a sheet, placed candles at his head and feet, and went to go see the trustee of the burial society, her face coursing with tears.

The trustee was delighted! He immediately counted out the hundred gulden and sent the gravediggers and a few members of the burial society to attend to the formalities.

Naturally, the funeral was no grand affair. Only a few people followed the procession to the edge of town. Beyond that point only proceeded the two gravediggers and their wagon.

When they passed a tavern, the gravediggers stopped the horse and went in for a drink, as gravediggers like to do. The "deceased" waited until the gravediggers were safely inside and then jumped out of the wagon and ran home.

By the time the gravediggers left the tavern, they were a little too drunk to notice anything awry. They settled back onto the wagon and drove off to the new cemetery.

When they arrived at the cemetery, they took down the casket—disaster! No corpse! Immediately they sobered up and decided to fill in the empty grave and not tell a soul.

That very day the "deceased" went out shopping for matzo, fish, meat, and wine, and the whole town was soon buzzing with the trick he'd played on the burial society.

Some time later another pauper in town died. Again only a few people attended the funeral, and the gravediggers were left alone with the wagon.

When they passed the tavern, they wanted to go in and have a drink.

"Now," said one of them to the other, "we know what precautions to take. This time the corpse won't run away!"

And so saying, they took out a heavy rope and tied it around the wagon.

A clever fellow stood nearby watching them and laughed, "How dumb could you be? The one who was alive—that's the one you should have tied up. Now this one is a real corpse, dead through and through—you don't need to tie him up. Regardless of any precautions you take, he's not going to run."

"You understand?" Reb Ayzl concluded. "It was the previous cantor whom you should have tied up with a contract. But this one, he's never leaving. Nobody's going to steal him away."

204

The cantor Tsalel Odesser was clever and sharp-tongued.

A youngster once asked him, "Tell me, Cantor, what's the reason you hold your finger under your chin when you sing?

"Oh?" replied Tsalel, feigning kind interest. "You want to know? Listen: for fifty years I've been holding my finger under my chin and I have no idea why. But you, you little squirt, want to know why in one second!"

205

When the Great Synagogue in Odessa was built, Tsalel was already an old man. When it was finished, everyone ran to go see it for themselves. It was a gorgeous building, and it had cost 300,000 rubles.

When Tsalel went inside, he stood in place and said, "You, Synagogue—what use is it to me that you're new and beautiful, while I'm old and broken-down? Better I be young and good-looking, and you be old and broken-down."

206

As an old man, when Tsalel had lost his teeth and his voice, he also lost his job as a major cantor. From then on, he began to lead services at smaller synagogues for the High Holidays.

One year, two synagogues both wanted to hire him. One belonged to the teamsters, and the other to the butchers. Tsalel agreed to lead the prayers for the butchers.

He was asked, "Cantor, why did you go to the butchers rather than the teamsters?"

"Well," answered Tsalel, "teamsters look their wares in the mouth, so I was afraid they wouldn't like what they'd see. But butchers check their wares from the back. From that vantage, I'll be a big hit."

207

Nisn Blumenthal, the cantor of Odessa, was an old-fashioned Jew. He didn't take to new ways—even when he was hired to be the cantor in the great modern Brody Synagogue. The synagogue's leaders had a very hard time convincing Blumenthal to wear a black cantor's robe and high cap. But above all he detested the title *Oberkantor*. In Odessa no one was allowed to address him as Oberkantor, only Herr Blumenthal, or simply Reb Nisn.

He once met Salomon Sulzer, the chief cantor of Vienna and the foremost leader of the movement to modernize synagogue music. Sulzer addressed him as "Herr Oberkantor." Blumenthal was furious.

"Are you ashamed of your trade?" asked Sulzer.

"Let me tell you a story," Blumenthal answered him. "There was once a famous thief in Odessa named Notke the Thief. Notke was a true master of his craft. He would pull off seemingly impossible heists that left everyone shaking their heads in wonder. There was no way to catch him.

"Notke the Thief used to complain, 'What good is my talent, when I belong to such an unimpressive guild? Any old pickpocket who lands a few bucks gets to call himself a thief.'"

209

Reb Yisroel Yofe, the cantor of Kalusz, was a learned and clever man. From time to time, he and his choir would go out on tour, as was common in those days.

One Friday, he realized he wasn't going to make it to a Jewish community in time for Shabbos. It was wintertime—when the day is short—and the road was bad, so he stopped at a nearby village where a Jewish innkeeper lived. He asked the innkeeper to let him and his party stay for Shabbos. The innkeeper, a coarse hick, told him to ride on.

"I don't mean to ask you to put us up for free," said Reb Yisroel. "I'll pay for food and lodging for me and my choir, whatever you ask."

The innkeeper wouldn't budge. He didn't want a cantor, and he didn't want a choir.

"Please," Reb Yisroel pleaded, "you can see that soon it will be Shabbos. There's only an hour of daylight left, and the road is bad—what city could I possibly reach in time? I'd have to stop and stay all night and all day out on the road or—God forbid—desecrate Shabbos."

The innkeeper softened up a bit and told him, "Any other Shabbos, I'd be happy to have you. But this Shabbos I can't."

"Why not?" asked Reb Yisroel.

"My head is broken into a thousand pieces," answered the innkeeper. "I feel ready to faint, and now on top of that I need to put up with you and your whole choir?"

"Was there, God forbid, some kind of incident?" Reb Yisroel inquired.

"I owe the landlord 1,000 gulden," the innkeeper complained, "and I don't have the money."

"That's all?" Reb Yisroel smiled. "I know exactly how you can handle that. You can rely on me."

Hearing that, the innkeeper was transformed. He immediately invited Reb Yisroel and all his choristers inside, gave them his best rooms, and took great care of them. That whole Shabbos he fed them his finest foods. He begged them to sing, too, and basked in their wonderful melodies.

After Shabbos, Reb Yisroel and the choristers prepared to set off. The innkeeper came up to Reb Yisroel and asked, "So, cantor—what is your advice?"

"Here's my advice," Reb Yisroel answered with a straight face. "Take 1,000 Russian pood [36,000 pounds] of wax and bring it to Kalusz. They have a shortage of wax there right now. You'll earn 1,000 gulden with no problem, and you'll be able to pay the landlord back."

"Where would I find wax?" asked the unsuspecting innkeeper. "And 1,000 Russian pood yet?"

"Oh?" Reb Yisroel feigned surprise. "You told me you didn't have any money, so I assumed you must have wax, and I had some advice for you. But you don't have any wax either, so I guess you're on your own!"

210

There were two cantors in Kherson: Pini Minkovsky and Halpern. Minkovsky was an old-fashioned Jew, a scholar and a Hasid. His specialty was the traditional Jewish style, but he tried his best to pray like the new cantors who had choirs. Halpern, on the other hand, was one of those new cantors, but he did his best to make his prayers sound more Jewish.

The richest man in town, Reb Zalmen Rozental, said, "We have two cantors. Neither of them can do what he wants. Halpern wishes to be a Jew, but can't; Minkovsky wants to be a Gentile, but can't."

685

Reb Meshulem Igra, the rabbi of Pressburg, was the rabbi of Tismenitz for a number of years before moving to Pressburg. A number of major communities offered him the rabbinic leadership of their towns due to his scholarly renown, but Reb Meshulem didn't want to leave Tismenitz.

When the Habsburg monarch Joseph II ordered that Jewish children be included in the military conscription, Tismenitz was told to supply a certain number of recruits. The heads of the community did the usual thing: They spared the more learned and wealthy boys, and they picked recruits from among the unpromising students and poor children.

Reb Meshulem made a big scene when he heard of this. He summoned the trustees and told them that this kind of discrimination was forbidden by Jewish law, that all Jews are equal. His proposal was a lottery—whoever's name came up, whether high or low, would become a soldier.

"And if they draw the name of my only son," he swore, "I'll personally see him off to service."

Still the trustees refused. At that, Reb Meshulem said, "The next offer I receive to leave Tismenitz for another post, I'll take."

When they heard about this in Pressburg, they immediately made him an offer.

687

Yudl Apotov was a self-made man who lived in Vilna. Like most nouveaux riches, he had a very high opinion of himself, did whatever he wanted, and ruled the city with a strong hand. Everyone in Vilna trembled at the mention of Apotov's name because he had friends high in the government. On top of that, he didn't mind dealing out a bit of violence—really a crude man.

Apotov once wanted to buy the state liquor license for himself, without asking permission from the community. When people found out about this, they were outraged: How could he just ignore the community like that? But it's Yudl Apotov—who knows what he might do if someone protested? He proceeded with the deal, paying a deposit to the government officials.

On the day when the license was scheduled to be sold, Vilna's preacher Reb Velvele called the heads of the community, including Apotov, to a meeting. Everyone began criticizing Apotov, but he didn't bat an eyelash. He wasn't interested in anybody's opinion and wasn't going to ask anybody's permission. Meanwhile, he kept looking at his pocket watch to make sure he wouldn't miss the auction and lose his deposit. When it was time to go, he went to the door—it was locked!

"Who did this?" Apotov angrily demanded.

"I did it, Reb Yudl," answered Reb Velvele. "I have the key, and you won't get it from me until the auction is over."

Apotov bit his lip and sat down. He lost his deposit, and he didn't get the license.

688

Reb Elye Kretinger, in addition to being pious and learned, was both worldly and rich. Nevertheless, he didn't approve of change and wouldn't suffer the abolition of even the most obscure Jewish custom.

One time in Kretinge, as could happen in any Jewish town, a dispute over being called to the Torah for an *aliye* turned physical. The secretary had called up someone for the seventh and final blessing, which is considered the least of the blessings. The person received it as a terrible insult. He said the blessing, but on the way back to his seat, he gave the secretary a slap in the face.

The whole town was shocked—to strike a fellow Jew, and in the synagogue at that!

The leaders of the community gathered at Reb Elye's house to discuss how to avoid such a sacrilegious incident in the future. Someone suggested that they abolish the system of designating certain *aliyes* as especially honored and just have everybody called up randomly.

"No," refused Reb Elye, "it's an old Jewish custom. It's obviously an insult and a sacrilege to hit a fellow Jew over an *aliye*, but if Jews stop seeking honor in our synagogues, it will be even worse. We'll wind up with no synagogues and no Jews. It's better to hold onto flawed customs and keep our synagogues with Jews inside them than to have faultless customs with no Jews and no synagogues in which to maintain them."

689

Moyshe Rozenson of Vilna was an avid modernizer, and because he preached the unification of Christians and Jews, he was suspected of being a Christian missionary. When he grew old, he ordered a marble headstone for his grave with a long, impressive inscription in fancy Hebrew. He knew very well that after he died, the community would not give him a respectable plot or erect such an imposing monument. He thought it over and decided to buy a plot while he was still alive.

He went to the community services office and said to the administrator, the famous modernizer Shmuel Yoysef Fuenn: "Reb Shmuel Yosl, I want to arrange a plot for myself—may I live to 120! And I want it to be in a prominent location."

"By all means," answered Fuenn with an air of perfect innocence.

"What will it cost me?" asked Rozenson.

"20,000 rubles," said Fuenn.

"20,000 rubles?!" thundered Rozenson. "You're trying to swindle me!" He pointed to the prices listed on the wall. "It clearly says that the first row only costs 400 rubles!"

"Well," smiled Fuenn, "that's the discount price—but to get it, first you have to die."

691

When the Bach served as rabbi in Krakow, he once traveled through a small nearby town and went to see the local rabbi. Just then, someone came in to see the rabbi with a question, to which he responded. The Bach didn't like his answer.

"You know," said the Bach, "I think the right thing to do would be for us to trade positions. You go to Krakow, and I'll stay here."

"What are you talking about, Rebbe?" wondered the rabbi. "I'm not in your league."

"Listen," answered the Bach, "in Krakow there are plenty of scholars who can answer questions like that. But here in your town, it looks like there's nobody who can."

694

When Rabbi Meir of Pressburg died and the community was looking for a replacement, everyone agreed that the offer should go to Reb Yitschok Charif, the rabbi of Sambur. They sent the proposed contract and a cover letter to Reb Yoyne, the head of the community in Sambur, asking him to convey it to Reb Yitschok. Reb Yoyne was a dear friend of Reb Yitschok, and he didn't want to see him leave Sambur. So he kept the letter to himself.

Several weeks passed with no reply from Reb Yitschok. The Pressburg community wrote to Sambur again, and again Reb Yoyne held onto it.

The folks in Pressburg assumed that Reb Yitschok didn't want to come there, so they decided to make an offer to Reb Meshulem Igra, the rabbi of Tismenitz. They sent him the contract with a letter explaining that they had twice made the offer to Reb Yitschok Charif, but had never heard back.

Reb Meshulem wanted to go to Pressburg, but since the offer had been made to Reb Yitschok first, he first traveled to Sambur to ask for his permission. Reb Yitschok warmly welcomed him, arranged a feast in his honor, and invited all of the town's leading luminaries.

Over the feast, Reb Meshulem explained why he had come, and asked Reb Yitschok whether he was absolutely certain he didn't want the Pressburg rabbinate. Reb Yitschok stared at him. He didn't know what to say. He had never received an offer from Pressburg.

Reb Yoyne covered his face with one hand, and with the other, silently drew out the two letters from his pocket and placed them on the table for Reb Yitschok to see.

"If so," said Reb Meshulem, "I won't go to Pressburg. The position is yours."

"No," said Reb Yitschok, "the Divine hand has shown us that you should be the rabbi of Pressburg."

And that's how Reb Meshulem became the rabbi of Pressburg.

706

Reb Naftoli Ropshitser once said: "I didn't want to be a rabbi. A rabbi has to flatter his congregation. I thought it over, and I decided to become a tailor. Then I realized that a tailor has to flatter his customers. Then I wanted to become a shoemaker, but a shoemaker also has to flatter his customers. How about a bathhouse keeper? Even they have to engage in flattery. So I asked myself: how is being a rabbi any worse? And I became a rabbi."

715

Reb Chatskl Ratner of Moliv was both wealthy and learned; he had actually written a few books. Being rich, he thought highly of himself, and he always made his opinions known when it came to communal matters, especially the rabbinate. He was a headache for every rabbi in town and even tormented the great Biblical commentator known as the Malbim.

Some time passed during which Moliv couldn't hire a rabbi. Anyone they tried to hire wasn't acceptable to Reb Chatskl. And if Reb Chatskl said no, that was that.

Reb Yoshe Ber Brisker commented on the situation: "Moliv won't be able to hire anybody, because Reb Chatskl wants a rabbi who knows less than him—and that kind of rabbi simply does not exist."

718

Reb Moyshe Kheyfets was the rabbi of Tshavus. He constantly had disputes with the community there. At one point, Pinsk was looking for a rabbi, and Reb Moyshe decided that was the place for him.

"Pinsk must really want me," he said. "After all, it's only logical: since Tshavus, which *doesn't* want me to be their rabbi, nevertheless wants me to be rabbi in Pinsk—then Pinsk, which *does* want me to be the rabbi of Tshavus, must certainly want me to be the rabbi in Pinsk."

720

Reb Meir, the rabbi of Slutsk, was an absolute genius and a righteous soul. When one of his granddaughters began attending the secular gymnasium, he resigned from the rabbinate.

"If I couldn't raise my own children properly, how can I guide a whole Jewish community?"

724

Reb Yankev Evan Fromer was the rabbi of Cleveland. He had terrible disputes with his congregants, as is often the case in a city. They wanted him to leave Cleveland, but naturally, he didn't want to go.

So Reb Yankev got up one day in shul and told them: "Listen, gentlemen. You should know once and for all that I am the Cleveland rabbi, and Cleveland is my city. If you like it, you can be members of the Cleveland community. If not, leave in good health. I'm not keeping you here."

728

When Reb Velvl, the author of *Maroys Hatsoyvos,* was the rabbi of Bialystok, there were two famous businessmen throughout Poland and Lithuania: Reb Ziml Epshteyn and Reb Kopl Halpern. They were partners who would take on large government contracts to build highways and bridges, thereby supporting hundreds of poor Jewish families. Reb Velvl knew and respected them for their generous philanthropy.

There once arose a business disagreement between the two men. They traveled to Bialystok so that Reb Velvl could resolve the dispute. He was known to be an absolute genius and a righteous soul.

Around 11:00 a.m., as Reb Velvl was teaching his classes, still in his tallis and tefillin, his assistant noticed a carriage stopping outside. The two great businessmen got out and headed toward the rabbi's house. The assistant ran to Reb Velvl and told him, gasping for air, "Rebbe, Reb Ziml Epshteyn and Reb Kopl Halpern are here!"

"Find out what brings them," Reb Velvl calmly replied.

The assistant soon came back and reported, "They want you to resolve a dispute."

"Call them in," said Reb Velvele. He let his tallis hang down over his eyes and asked the rabbinical judge to sit next to him.

When the magnates walked in, Reb Velvele gave them no greeting and didn't invite them to sit down; he didn't even look at them. He simply said, "Ziml and Kopl, whichever one of you is the plaintiff, speak first."

The rich men got nervous. They hadn't expected such a cold welcome, being addressed by their first names, without the honorific "Reb."

"I'm the plaintiff," Reb Ziml barely managed to stammer.

"Speak. Let me hear your claim," said Reb Velvele.

Reb Ziml was crestfallen. He briefly summarized his claim.

"Kopl. Now you," Reb Velvele commanded.

When he'd heard both sides, Reb Velvele sent them out and talked it over with the judge. When the two had reached agreement, he sent his assistant to call Reb Ziml and Reb Kopl back in. "According to the Torah, the ruling must be such-and-such. Ziml, do you accept it?"

"Yes, Rebbe," answered Reb Ziml.

"Kopl, do you accept it?" Reb Velvele then asked.

"Yes, Rebbe," answered Reb Kopl.

Reb Velvele took the tallis off his head then and greeted them: "*Sholem aleykhem*, Reb Ziml! *Sholem aleykhem*, Reb Kopl!"

And he ordered his assistant to set out refreshments for his honored guests.

731

The following dispute was once brought to Reb Berish Meisels, the rabbi of Warsaw.

A certain Jew passed away in the Jewish hospital in Warsaw. His heirs knew that he possessed a large sum of money. They began to search for it, but they looked everywhere and didn't find it. Suspicion fell on the servant who had been close to the dying man. They interrogated the servant, but he absolutely denied knowing anything about it. They brought him to the rabbi.

Reb Berish asked him: "Do you deny taking the money?"

"I deny it," the servant insisted.

"If so," answered Reb Berish, "you'll have to shake hands with the deceased."

The servant was rather distressed, but he rallied and said: "Yes, Rebbe, I'll shake his hand."

Reb Berish called a few trusted men into a side room and said: "Go to the hospital. Somebody who's living should pretend to be a corpse, and when the servant takes his hand, he should hold onto the servant's hand for a while and not let go."

And so it was arranged. They had someone lie down on the ground, covered him with a sheet, and placed lit candles at his feet, like a corpse.

A while later, the servant was brought in. He was told to approach the deceased and shake his hand.

The servant approached and took the hand. When he wanted to withdraw his own hand, he couldn't, because the "corpse" wouldn't let go. The servant grew pale as a sheet, nearly fainted, and began shouting: "*Gevalt!* Don't hurt me! I'll return the money!"

735

A young scholar once came to Reb Zalmen of Mariampol to seek rabbinic ordination. Reb Zalmen spent some time discussing Talmud and the legal codes with him—no question, he was a fine young scholar, worthy of serving as a rabbi.

Reb Zalmen asked him, "Do you know the fifth section of the *Shulchan Aruch*? A rabbi absolutely has to know it."

The young man stared at him.

"Rebbe," wondered the young man, "I've never heard that there was a fifth section of the *Shulchan Aruch*."

"That fifth part," said Reb Zalmen, "begins with the words from our morning prayers, *l'oylem yehey odam...* you should always be a mentsh."

740

A Gentile once came to see Reb Elye Chaim Lodzher seeking a confidential audience with "Mister Rabbi." Reb Elye Chaim brought him into his private study. The man confided in him:

"Me, I'm from Lodz, the Balut neighborhood. I was involved in the uprising against the Russians. I kept the treasury for the whole region. When the uprising was quashed, I still had about 8,000 rubles. I didn't know what to do with it, so I buried it in the cellar. I guarded that money with my life and didn't tell a soul it was there. From time to time, I would go down into the cellar by myself, counting the money and putting more away there from my own earnings. Years went by. Just now, I went to the cellar, and the money wasn't there. I nearly fainted. I began crying, shouting, and tearing the hair from my head. The neighbors gathered, but no one could help me. The money just wasn't there."

"Do you suspect anyone?" asked Reb Elye Chaim.

"I really don't know, Mister Rabbi. It's like this: A Jewish carpenter lives in part of my house. He's a poor tradesman and he's always in debt. He and his family were always dressed in rags—it broke your heart to see them. Suddenly the carpenter seems to be doing fine. He got new furniture, new clothes, and started living like a rich guy. So..."

"Did anyone ask the carpenter where his new money came from?" pressed Reb Elye Chaim.

"Yes," answered the Gentile, "several of our neighbors asked. He says that his wife's great uncle died in London and left him a big inheritance. But I can't rest. I'm going out of my mind. So I'm asking Mister Rabbi for his advice."

"Come back tomorrow around this time," said Reb Elye Chaim.

When the man left, Reb Elye Chaim sent for the carpenter, who promptly appeared.

"'I've heard that you're suddenly doing well, that you've got plenty of money," said Reb Elye Chaim. "Why haven't you come to give me a nice donation for one of our local charities?"

The man didn't know what to say for a while, but then he spoke up: "Of course you're right, Rebbe, it just slipped my mind. But it's not too late."

"Apparently your uncle was very rich?" Reb Elye Chaim asked.

"Yes," said the carpenter, "he was loaded."

"Did he leave money to anybody else?" continued Reb Elye Chaim.

"Yes... uh, no," stammered the carpenter.

By this point Reb Elye Chaim understood that the story about an inheritance was suspicious.

"Listen," he said quietly, "I sent for you for your own good, to save you from disaster. I've been informed that you're paying people with counterfeit money. You know where that can land you."

The Jew grew pale. It must be that his Gentile neighbor was a forger.

"Rebbe," he trembled, "I'll tell you the whole truth. I found the money buried in the cellar. Later I found out that my Gentile neighbor had buried it there. Who could imagine it was forged?"

"You run home," said Reb Elye Chaim, "and bring back all of that money you have left."

The carpenter ran home and brought back a sack of coins.

"From now on you should remember," scolded Reb Elye Chaim, "that you can't take what doesn't belong to you. The coin is true. But it's not yours."

The next day the Gentile got back his money.

741

During all the years that Reb Chaim was the rabbi of Brisk, he almost never answered questions on Jewish law. He had scholars in his court who would answer the people's questions.

Once Reb Chaim came in from the street and met a girl on her way out, carrying a chicken.

"Excuse me," he said, "show me the bird."

Reb Chaim examined the bird from all sides—there was no hint of anything wrong with it. He went into the courtroom and asked: "How did you rule on the chicken?"

"Kosher, of course," he was answered. "There's no question at all about it."

"Go home," Reb Chaim said to the girl, "and bring me the other chicken."

The girl went home and returned with another chicken. The other chicken did in fact have a problem, and it actually turned out not to be kosher.

Everyone was amazed—it was clearly a wonder.

"It's quite simple," Reb Chaim explained. "No one is going to come consult about a chicken that's perfectly kosher. So I realized that they had probably slaughtered two chickens, and one of them presented a problem, but when they sent someone to ask, they accidentally sent the kosher one instead."

752

Reb Moyshe Yitschok, the Kelmer Maggid, once visited Dubeln, a city near Riga, where people came every summer to bathe in the sea. A number of Jews from Riga would spend every Shabbos of the season at Dubeln.

On Shabbos morning in shul, Reb Moyshe Yitschok noticed a number of men praying without a tallis, which they had apparently been too lazy to pack and carry. He got up on the platform and said, "Listen, gentlemen, to the story I will tell:

> I spent last Shabbos in Riga. I went to see someone and was told he wasn't at home.
> "Where is he?" I asked.
> "Gone to Dubeln," they told me.
> Suddenly I heard a strange weeping emanating from another room. I walked in—it was empty. But a tallis bag was hanging on the wall, and I could hear the tallis crying.
> "Tallis, tallis," I asked, "why are you crying?"
> "Why shouldn't I be crying?" said the tallis. "When my owner went off to Dubeln, he made sure to take all his gold and silver, but he left me behind."
> "Don't cry, tallis," I told it. "In return, your owner will one day be compelled to take a much longer journey. He'll have to leave the gold and silver behind, and the only thing he'll take along is you."

754

Reb Moyshe Yitschok, the Kelmer Maggid, once traveled to Posvil, a small town in the Vilna region. He went to see the rabbi to find out how Yiddishkeit was faring in this town. The rabbi told him that he had presided over a dispute just that day, and the party he had deemed at fault refused to pay up.

That Shabbos, as Reb Moyshe Yitschok was about to climb up onto the platform in the synagogue to preach to the congregants, he suddenly stopped, and then began speaking softly, as if he were having a private argument with somebody, and concluded loudly:

"But we're in Posvil!"

And only then did he climb up.

"My honored hosts," he began, "let me tell you a story."

While I was on my way here, I ran into Satan.

"'Good morning, Kelmer,' he said, 'where are you headed?'

"'I'm on my way to Posvil.'

"'What are you going to do there?'

"'The same as I do in every town. I'll give sermons, rebuke them for their sins, make them repent and live more piously.'

"'You should know,' he warned me, 'that you're not permitted to speak in Posvil. Posvil is my town.'

"'What do you mean, your town? Posvil is a Jewish town like any other.'

"With that, I wished to proceed on my way, but he wouldn't leave me alone. Posvil belongs to him, he insisted, and I mustn't speak there. Finally, he suggested that we go to a rabbi and have him settle this.

"Look, if you're summoned to a rabbinical court, you have to go. We went to see the rabbi, he heard us both out, and Satan won. The decision was that I mustn't speak in Posvil.

"Now just a few minutes ago, I was on my way to the platform to speak, and I saw that Satan was there.

"'What's going on?' he complained. 'I won the judgment. You heard the rabbi—you're not allowed to speak here!'

"Well, he had me dead to rights—until suddenly I remembered that we're in Posvil, and in Posvil, they don't follow any rabbi's rulings. So I just ignored him, and went right up onto the platform."

765

There was a cantor in Vilna named Yoshe Goldes. He had a sharp mind and frequently came up with witty sayings.

"Reb Yoshe," someone once asked, "people say that all cantors are fools. But you're a cantor and a very intelligent man."

"Eh," answered Yoshe, "The Talmud says you can't prove anything from the behavior of a fool, so what can you prove based on me?"

768

Cantor Kuper was once asked: "Why are there so many cantors in America?"

"That's how it's always been with the Jews," he answered. "When Moses was at home in Egypt, he was a stammerer who could barely speak, may it not happen to us. But as soon as he crossed the ocean, well aha!—'then sang Moses.'"

Study and Prayer

211

The Gaon of Vilna almost never left his house. He always sat in his room, windows closed and shuttered even by day. From morning to night he would sit, studying and praying by the light of a single candle.

One of the Gaon's sisters came to see him for the first time in many years. She barely managed to convince his household to let her in to see him.

When she entered his room, the Gaon turned his face to her, lowered his tallis from his head, and said, "In the World to Come, we'll have plenty of time to see each other. Here I need the time to study."

213

Reb Chaim Volozhiner had a saying: "Sometimes you have to study one folio of Talmud for ten hours, and sometimes you have to study ten folios in one hour."

215

Reb Chaim Volozhiner, as everybody knows, was the founder and leader of the Volozhin Yeshiva. The expenses were high right from the start, and money was always tight.

Once during the Napoleonic wars, a Jew came to see Reb Chaim and begged him to take 800 rubles and keep the money safe for him. The man explained that he lived very far away and had come to deliver supplies to the military. Now that he had completed his business, he wanted to go home, but he was afraid of carrying cash on his person during such uncertain times. He hoped Reb Chaim would do him a favor and keep the money until he was next able to return. He gave Reb Chaim permission to use the money for the yeshiva's expenses in the meantime.

Reb Chaim took the money and used it for the yeshiva. A year passed, another year, then three—the man didn't come back for his money. Finally, after the third year, he returned. He went to see the secretary of the yeshiva and explained who he was and that he had come to get his money. The secretary went to Reb Chaim and informed him that the man who had loaned them 800 rubles had returned. That was an enormous sum in those days, and there wasn't a cent in the yeshiva's coffers. There was no chance of borrowing it, either. All of Volozhin put together wouldn't be able to provide a sum that big. Reb Chaim quickly thought it over and answered, "Go tell him that tomorrow before the afternoon prayers he'll get his money."

Reb Itsele, Reb Chaim's son—at that time still a young man—was astonished. Where would his father get such a huge sum so quickly? But he didn't say anything. He waited to see what would happen.

All day, Reb Chaim kept to his usual routine. He busied himself with study and prayer, with the business of the yeshiva, and he didn't give a single thought to finding the money. The next day—the same thing: Reb Chaim prayed and delivered his lecture as usual, without a hint of worry. Reb Itsele couldn't believe it.

That afternoon, the local nobleman came to Reb Chaim with a request: He had a thousand rubles in banknotes and wanted to exchange them for coins. And since the rabbi regularly received donations from all over the world, he wanted the rabbi to take his thousand rubles in banknotes and pay it back in coin over time.

After seeing the nobleman off, Reb Chaim gave the Jew his 800 rubles and blessed him for granting the yeshiva the use of his money.

216

When Reb Chaim Volozhiner grew old, he handed over the task of teaching the regular Talmud lessons to his son, Reb Itsele. Reb Chaim would stop in at the yeshiva from time to time, stand behind the furnace where nobody could see him, and listen to Reb Itsele's lesson.

Once, during the lesson, he heard Reb Itsele cite one of his questions on the text: "My father, may he be well, here asks the following..." and briefly summarize the question. Then his son began to provide a solution of his own, very precisely and at great length, bringing various citations as evidence, as Reb Itsele knew how to do.

When the lesson ended, Reb Chaim came out from behind the furnace, approached the table and said: "Children, I'll tell you a story.

> When I used to travel around raising money for the yeshiva, I once arrived at an inn on Friday afternoon. And since it was wintertime and the days were short, I couldn't travel any further, and had to stay at the inn.
>
> Before candle-lighting, I saw the innkeeper's wife groom the hair of her two daughters in honor of Shabbos. To one of them she devoted a scant minute—wash, comb, done. The other girl she washed, soaped, groomed, combed her hair for a long time—really paid attention to her. What do you suppose was the difference between the two children?"
>
> "Papa, you are supposing," Reb Itsele understood immediately, "that one child was her own but the other a stepchild. No, both of them were hers and they were equally beloved and precious. But one child was already clean, so her mother didn't need

to devote a lot of time to her. One quick wash was enough. The other child was dirty and scratched up, so her mother had to wash and groom her for a long time before she got clean."

220

When he was a boy, Reb Mendl of Vitebsk studied under Reb Ber, the Maggid of Mezritsh. He was a capable and diligent student.

One Shabbos afternoon, the Maggid saw the boy walking around the room with his hat at a rakish angle, looking quite pleased with himself.

"Mendl," he asked, "how many folios of Talmud did you study today?"

"Six," replied the boy.

"Oho!" replied the Maggid. "If from six folios your hat is ready to lean to the side, how many will it take until your hat falls clean off?"

222

When Moses Mendelssohn had gained renown as a scholar and philosopher, the members of the Berlin Academy elected him a member. The German Kaiser, Frederick the Great, refused to permit the appointment and crossed Mendelssohn's name off the list.

When Mendelssohn found out, he smiled and said, "I'd rather the scholars choose me and the Kaiser refuse, than to have the Kaiser choose me and the scholars refuse."

225

Reb Moyshe Sofer, known as the Chasam Sofer, used to say: "It's no wonder that Moyshe Rabeynu, our great master Moses, was Moyshe Rabeynu. Look, if I had the Teacher he had, I'd be just like him. That being said, why don't I have the Teacher he had? Because I'm not Moyshe Rabeynu."

226

Reb Akiva Eiger once came to Warsaw to visit his son, Reb Shloyme Eiger. Since Reb Akiva was spending too much time lost in study to the point that it was harming his health, his son decided to distract him a bit with worldly interests. So he took his father to the museum in Warsaw.

When they got there, the museum guard graciously welcomed them and offered Reb Akiva a fine chair. Reb Akiva sat down and immediately became lost in thought about matters of Torah. After he'd been sitting there for some time, he looked up with a start and asked his son, "Eh? Why aren't they bringing in the baby?"

He had completely forgotten where he was, and thought that he was a sandek at a bris, sitting on Elijah's chair.

227

Reb Boruch Kosover once entered his study house. He saw the young men engaged in clever disputes, each one trying to show off his learning and one-up the other.

"Wow!" said Reb Boruch. "This study house is full of Torah!"

This pleased the youngsters. Reb Boruch clearly had a high opinion of them!

"Please understand me," said Reb Boruch. "If you're studying for its own sake, without ulterior motives, the Torah rises up almost to the level of the Almighty. The study house is left empty. But if you're studying just to show off, the Torah remains trapped here below. That's why our study house is full of Torah."

229

Reb Boruch Laypniker, Reb Chaim Sanzer's father-in-law, once explained the subtle difference between two similar cases of Torah law in such a way that only an advanced scholar could appreciate. He concluded, "Of course, it's an extremely fine distinction."

"Yes," smiled Reb Chaim, "so fine that the first time it gets repeated, nothing will be left to tell."

232

Once, when Reb Mendele Kotsker had already become a famous rebbe, he visited his hometown of Bilgoraj. He went to visit his first master, from whom he had learned his letters as a small child. His second childhood teacher, who had taught him Torah and Talmud, scolded him: "Rebbe, why didn't you come to see me first? I taught you more, after all."

"It's like this," Reb Mendele answered. "You taught me the sort of things that I can never be entirely certain of. As soon as one person says this is the plain meaning, another comes in and disagrees. But when it comes to the alphabet that my first teacher taught me, I'm certain that aleph is aleph and beys is beys!"

233

A young Hasid once came to visit Reb Mendele Kotsker. "How are your studies going?" asked Reb Mendele.

"Rebbe," came the proud reply, "I've finished the entire Talmud."

"Is that so?" returned Reb Mendele. "But is the Talmud finished with you?"

235

Reb Ayzl Kharif had a sharp tongue and wasn't afraid to tell anyone what he thought of them, straight to their face. Other rabbis watched out for him like fire.

A rabbi once came to visit him. The rabbi knew who Reb Ayzl was, and he came prepared to deliver an impressive, learned discourse. He had prepared an interesting and difficult problem along with a solid and incisive solution, weaving together breadth and depth of scholarship.

As they sat discussing Torah, the rabbi posed his question. Reb Ayzl heard the question and asked, "Well, what's your solution?"

The rabbi felt proud. If Reb Ayzl was curious about the resolution, it meant the problem itself was a good one. He began to lay out the solution, lavishing it with his breadth of knowledge, displaying his insight, and cutting through seemingly impossible obstacles—a neat piece of scholarship.

Reb Ayzl listened and asked, "So what's the problem?"

"May you be well, Rebbe," the rabbi wondered. "Obviously, once the solution is offered, there's no more problem."

"As I see it," Reb Ayzl said, "sometimes, when you have a really neat solution, you come up with some kind of problem that will allow you to present the solution. But when the solution is ten times worse than the problem—I have to ask, what's the problem?"

239

Reb Yoshe Ber was once told that his son, Reb Chaimke, was impressed with his own scholarship and had become a little full of himself.

Reb Yoshe Ber sent for him and said to him, "Chaimke, teach me something new."

As soon as Reb Chaimke began to speak, Reb Yoshe Ber interrupted him: "No doubt your question was going to be thus-and-such, and you would answer it like-this-and-that."

"That's right, Father," responded Reb Chaim.

"Teach me something else new," Reb Yoshe Ber said to him.

Reb Chaimke began sharing a more profound analysis. But Reb Yoshe Ber interrupted him once again: "No doubt such-and-such is the question you intend to pose, and you'll answer it in such-and-such a way."

Reb Chaimke waited.

"Come on, teach me some real Torah," said Reb Yoshe Ber. "Let's see what you can do."

Reb Chaimke considered for a while and then came up with an

even more impressive insight, a real stroke of genius, and began to relate it, thinking this time that his father wouldn't beat him.

But Reb Yoshe Ber didn't let him talk for long. He interrupted once again, "Why keep talking? I'll tell you what you're thinking."

At this, Reb Chaim fell silent. "You see, my child," said Reb Yoshe Ber, "knowing how to learn isn't as easy as you think."

"I'll tell you, Father," answered Reb Chaim. "In the new editions of the Talmud, the comments of Reb Akiva Eiger are printed in the margins. Inside the text of the Talmud itself, at the point where Reb Akiva Eiger has a new insight, there's just an asterisk meaning 'take a look at the comments of Reb Akiva Eiger.' Scholars who know Reb Akiva Eiger's approach don't always need to look at the notes themselves. As soon as they see an asterisk, they know what Reb Akiva Eiger would have to say. Nevertheless, Reb Akiva Eiger is still Reb Akiva Eiger.

"It's the same with me, Father: you know my approach to learning. As soon as I start talking, you can see what I'm thinking. But does that mean that my ideas aren't really new?"

241

When a youngster would come to Volozhin to study, after he completed the entrance exam, Reb Hersh Leyb would ask him, "So do you really want to study?"

"Yes," the boy would answer.

"Will you devote yourself to Torah study day and night?"

"Yes."

"Every hour of your life?"

"Yes!"

"But do you know what that really means?" Reb Hersh Leyb would ask and then immediately explain: "It means eat when you're supposed to, sleep when you're supposed to, and study when you're supposed to."

243

While Reb Yitschok Elchonon and his wife lived with her father in Vilkovisk, they deposited for safekeeping their marriage dowry, all 300 rubles of it, with the richest man in town. One day the man went suddenly bankrupt. Reb Yitschok Elchonon's wife went to see the rich man and pleaded with him to give her the money—it was everything she had. But the rich man refused to answer her.

"Let your husband come instead," he said.

She went home, where Reb Yitschok Elchonon was sitting and studying. She tried to convince him to go to the rich man himself: maybe he could recoup some of the money. Reb Yitschok Elchonon went right on studying, as if he didn't hear a word. At that, his wife began crying. Meanwhile, her father came in.

"What happened?" he asked.

His daughter explained that she was trying to get her husband to go get some of the money back, but it was like talking to the wall. All he knew how to do was to sit over his books.

Her father gave her two slaps and shouted, "You leave him to his studies, hear? One minute of his learning is worth more to me than the entire dowry."

246

The famous scholar Reb Yeruchem Leyb, The Gadol of Minsk, was born the son of a tailor.

He was once sitting with two other rabbis, both of whom stemmed from rabbinic families. They wished to tease this upstart, so they began to boast of their fathers' teachings.

One said, "My esteemed father, of blessed memory, posed such-and-such impossible problem and provided such-and-such brilliant solution."

And the other, "My holy father, of blessed memory, taught this-and-that."

"And my father the *tailor*, of blessed memory," responded Reb

Yeruchem Leyb, "said that worn-out hand-me-downs are worthless, and there's nothing like working with new cloth." And with that, Reb Yeruchem Leyb began to expound an insightful discourse of his own design.

251

Professor Solomon Schechter, the head of the Jewish Theological Seminary, had a quick wit and a sharp tongue.

In the middle of one of his lectures, one of the students blurted out something not too bright.

"Well," Schechter said in English, "you are a 'great nation.'"

"What do you mean?" asked the student.

"Very simple," smiled Schechter, "you're a '*goy godel*.'"

252

The Hebrew poet Chaim Nachman Bialik was once sitting in the study hall in Zhitomir, reading an old Hebrew book.

Though still a young man, he had already suspended his studies at the great yeshiva of Volozhin and was no longer a full-time denizen of the study hall.

Everyone else in the study hall was surprised to see him there.

One elderly man was curious enough to ask. He approached Bialik, glanced at the book and asked, "Chaim Nachman, what are you looking at here?"

"What I see here," answered Bialik, "is not what you see."

254

Reb Levi Yitschok of Berdichev once saw a Jewish coachman standing in his tallis and tefillin, praying as he greased the wheels of his wagon.

Reb Levi Yitschok lifted his eyes to heaven and said, "See, Lord, what a precious people Jews are. Here's a simple Jew, and even while he greases the wheels, he prays to You."

258

Reb Leyzer Yitschok, the son-in-law of Reb Itsele Volozhiner, noticed that a fellow in the yeshiva prayed too fast. He summoned him to his office and spoke about the importance of prayer. He explained that one must slowly and carefully concentrate on it, just as if one were counting money.

"But as you know, Rebbe," answered the fellow, "if you drive too slowly the street brats jump onto the wagon. But if you drive fast, they can't get on. If you pray quickly, then there's no time for wicked thoughts."

"My concern, you brat," smiled Reb Leyzer Yitschok, "is that you pray so fast, you miss the wagon entirely."

260

It is said that Reb Pinches, author of the *Haflo'oh*, was up studying one winter night, well past midnight, while outside it was deadly cold and snowing. Suddenly, he heard a knock on the door and a pleading voice, "Have mercy, let a Jew come in."

Reb Pinches opened the door, and a man staggered in, frozen to the bone and covered with snow, practically half-dead. Reb Pinches sat him down near the warm oven, gave him something hot to drink and something to eat, and eventually the man revived.

He begged Reb Pinches' forgiveness for knocking on the door in the middle of the night. He explained that he was a merchant on his way to the fair, but he had barely made it to town. This house had been the only one with a flame still seen burning through the window.

As they chatted, he said to Reb Pinches, "You see, rabbi, that I don't have any pleasure from this world. I lead a dog's life, always on the road, through cold and heat. Will I at least get to enjoy the World to Come?"

"Look," said Reb Pinches, "you already struggle so hard for the pleasures of this world, but don't get to enjoy any of them—what makes you think you'll enjoy the World to Come, that you don't work for at all?"

And others finish the story like this: "If that's how it worked, then your horse would deserve it more than you. He's still outside, suffering in the cold."

261

Reb Shneur Zalmen of Liadi, the first Lubavitcher Rebbe, used to say in moments of spiritual ecstasy: "Master of the Universe, I don't want your Paradise, I don't want your World to Come, I want You alone!"

266

As everybody knows, a Jewish government informant once ratted on Reb Yisroel Rizhiner to the authorities, and they sent him to prison. When Reb Yisroel got out, he said:

"I'd never understood why the Evil Inclination is called 'King, Old Man, and Fool.' King, I could understand—he rules over humankind. Old man, sure—he's been visiting each of us since the day we were born. But why a fool? I figured it out in prison. While I was locked up in the cell, the Evil Inclination sat beside me the whole time and stuck to me like a fly to honey.

"'So,' I said to him, 'you really are an idiot, aren't you? It's perfectly understandable for me to sit confined here, unable to see the light of day—I have no choice. But *you*?'"

269

Reb Leybele Chosid was extremely careful with his speech. He counted every word to make sure he didn't stumble into a falsehood, evil gossip, or other forbidden language.

A young man from his town once went to pay him a visit. After a while, the young man excused himself, saying, "Rebbe, no doubt you're very busy."

"How do you know?" Reb Leybele asked him.

"I just figured you must be," the young man answered.

"Yet you said 'no doubt,'" Reb Leybele scolded him. "A Jew must guard his tongue."

270

When Reb Zundl Salanter was studying in Volozhin, his fellows at the yeshiva noticed that every morning, he would go out for a stroll in the Gentile neighborhood while smoking his pipe, like a real aristocrat, not like a proper yeshiva student. The rosh yeshiva got wind of this, and he sent for Reb Zundl to ask him if it was true.

"Yes, Rebbe," answered Reb Zundl, "it's true. I found out that a lot of Jews in town buy forbidden bread from Gentile bakers. So every morning I go to the Gentile bakeries and ask for a flame to light my pipe. Meanwhile I manage to toss a stick into the oven—and so I make sure Jews are eating acceptable bread, considered baked by a Jew."

274

Reb Yisroel Salanter once went to a shoemaker to get his shoes mended. It was evening, and the shoemaker was working by the light of a candle that was about to burn itself out.

"A shame," said Reb Yisroel, "you won't have time to finish."

"No, Rebbe," answered the shoemaker. "As long as the candle burns, I can still mend."

"You're right!" Reb Yisroel passionately exclaimed, and he began walking around the room, humming to himself in his own pious melody, "As long as the candle burns, I can still mend."

276

Reb Yitschok Meir of Ger was once told that there was a machine that could heat up the mikveh.

"No wonder," smiled Reb Yitschok Meir. "Hot generations need cold mikvehs. Cold generations need hot mikvehs."

277

In a tiny hamlet near Wilkomir, there lived a Jew. His behavior was coarse and rude. Everyone, including other country Jews, called him "Despicable Leybe."

The rabbi of Wilkomir, Reb Shloymele the Great, was once heading home to Wilkomir during the winter. The road was poor and it was a Friday, and Reb Shloyme realized that he wouldn't make it home for Shabbos. He told the coachman to turn aside at the nearest village, to the home of the only Jew who lived there, Despicable Leybe. When he arrived, Leybe at first tried to discourage him from staying there. How could the rabbi spend Shabbos with such a lowlife as himself? Better he should drive on a bit. A ways further on there was a Jewish inn, where he could keep Shabbos properly. But Reb Shloymele answered that he never traveled on Friday after midday, so he would have to stay at Leybe's house.

That evening, Reb Shloymele noticed that this country Jew didn't have bad manners. On the contrary, he was punctilious in his attention to ritual detail, like a scholar. Reb Shloymele asked Leybe a few questions that were so simple and friendly that Leybe couldn't help but answer. The conversation took off and the rabbi quickly realized that Despicable Leybe was in fact quite a sharp scholar who was modest to a fault. Leybe begged Reb Shloymele not to tell anyone, because he didn't want it to be general knowledge.

Some years later, as Reb Shloymele was leaving the study house, he came upon a funeral.

"Who died?" he asked.

"A simple, country Jew," was the answer. "Despicable Leybe."

When Reb Shloymele heard the name, he tore his clothes in mourning and ordered the funeral procession to come to the study house so that he could personally deliver a eulogy. He revealed Despicable Leybe's true identity and the whole town joined the funeral procession.

278

A traveling charitable collector once came to see Reb Yoshe Ber Brisker on Friday afternoon. Reb Yoshe Ber invited him to stay over for Shabbos.

Before candle-lighting, Reb Yoshe Ber said to his guest, "Please do me a favor and lend me five kopeks."

The guest gave him five kopeks.

On Saturday night after Havdalah, Reb Yoshe Ber returned the five kopeks to the collector. The guest noticed that they were the same coins he had given the rabbi.

"Please don't be offended, Rebbe," he said. "But may I ask you why you had me lend you five kopeks? I see that you didn't even exchange them for other coins."

"It's like this," answered Reb Yoshe Ber. "You're a traveler, always on the road. When will you ever get the chance to perform the mitzvah of providing a free loan? Who's going to try to borrow money from somebody who's just passing through town? So I wanted to help you perform the mitzvah."

279

Reb Yoshe Ber had no patience for displays of ignorant piety. He once saw someone pouring out two full pitchers of water to wash their hands before eating.

"That poor Jew," smiled Reb Yoshe Ber. "He's pouring out all his fear of God into the slop bucket."

281

During the time the Vilna Gaon was traveling incognito as an itinerant beggar, he was once walking from one town to another when a Jewish coachman passed by. The coachman saw a Jew on foot carrying his satchel on his back, so he asked, "Where are you going, Reb Yid?"

"To town," the walker answered.

"Climb on up," said the coachman. "I'll take you there."

The Gaon got onto the wagon and they rode on. The day grew warmer, and the Gaon took off his coat and sat there wearing his tefillin and studying Torah, as was the Gaon's way.

Along the way, the coachman said, "Reb Yid, I'm so sleepy, I want to lie down in the wagon a bit. Could you do me a favor? Sit up here in front and take the whip and reins. The horses know the road like a pious Jew knows how to pray: they don't need a great sage to direct them."

Without saying a word, the Gaon switched places with the coachman to drive the horses. It was a chance to help another Jew.

And that's how they arrived in town.

Just as they got to town, they were met by a Jew who had been to Vilna and recognized the Gaon. He saw the Gaon sitting like a coachman and someone else riding as a passenger. Breathless, he ran off to the marketplace and began shouting at the top of his lungs, "Jews, Moshiach has arrived! Moshiach has arrived!"

People gathered from all over town. They asked, "What happened?"

"Moshiach has arrived," the Jew panted. "And he's coming here."

What could the others do but stare at him and wonder whether he was crazy or just plain witless?

"With my own eyes I saw it," the man solemnly swore. "A wagon riding into town, and none other but the Vilna Gaon driving the horses. So who could be his passenger if not Moshiach?"

Meanwhile, the wagon reached the marketplace. The townspeople were shocked and stunned. There on the coachman's seat sat the

Gaon, wearing his tallis and tefillin and holding the whip and reins.

They ran to the wagon, looked inside and saw... the town coachman. He lay there, happily snoring away.

286

The two saints, the brothers Reb Elimelech and Reb Zushe, famously wandered from land to land incognito, walking the roads like two simple paupers.

They once arrived at a country inn just when the local villagers were celebrating a wedding. The two brothers went in and sat in a corner, like paupers. Reb Elimelech sat by the wall and Reb Zushe sat facing the crowd.

When the locals had gotten deep into their cups, they decided to have fun with the two beggars in the corner. They grabbed Reb Zushe, who was sitting closer to them, laid him out on the ground, and took turns, each giving him a solid punch, as though it was all a joke. After every dance, they repeated this whole process.

When this "joke" had been repeated a few times, Reb Elimelech said to Reb Zushe, "My dear Zushe, why should you receive all the blows, and none for me? Let's switch places, and next time they'll do it to me."

Reb Zushe agreed. While the drunken celebrants danced, they switched places: Reb Zushe sat by the wall and Reb Elimelech sat nearer the crowd.

The next dance finished, and one of the partygoers called out to the others, "Brothers, it's unjust for us to pick on the same one every time. Let's get the other one, who's sitting by the wall. Let him feel our fists too, so he'll remember that he was at the wedding."

So once again they grabbed Reb Zushe, threw him to the ground and beat him.

When Reb Zushe got up and sat back down next to Reb Elimelech, he said, "You see, my dear brother, when you're the one who's fated to be struck, there's no escaping it."

282

As is well known, the Shages Aryeh spent time in self-imposed exile. He wandered from town to town, wearing a long linen caftan bound with a rope. To the rope he tied a pot and a spoon, and he carried a bundle on his back. Wherever he arrived, he would ask to have some of his own barley groats cooked in his own pot. Since he was very careful to avoid eating *kemakh yoshen,* a rule that many others did not observe, he wouldn't eat anyone else's food and even avoided their utensils.

Once he arrived at Breslau, where Reb Yeshaye Pik, the author of *Mesores Hashas,* was the rabbi. Reb Yeshaye was a rich Jew who lived lavishly. The Shages Aryeh came to Reb Yeshaye's house and rudely instructed the rebbetzin: "Here's some buckwheat groats and a pot, so cook something up for me."

Reb Yeshaye's wife stared at him. At Reb Yeshaye's home, in Breslau, this kind of behavior was unheard of. Moreover, the Shages Aryeh had a strange appearance: a head as big as a bucket, with a broad nose and a pair of fiery eyes.

The rabbi's wife went into Reb Yeshaye's office and told him that a strange Jew had come to the house—a pauper, evidently somewhat deranged—demanding that she cook his own food for him in his own pot.

The Shages Aryeh walked through rooms richly decorated with beautiful furniture, the likes of which he had never seen before. Reb Yeshaye's office was also richly appointed.

Reb Yeshaye started up a conversation with his guest, asking him where he had come from and where he was headed. The Shages Aryeh immediately rejoindered with a scholarly question, and most likely a tough one, as was the Shages Aryeh's way. Reb Yeshaye spent a few minutes in concentration and came up with a solution. The Shages Aryeh liked the answer.

"You really amaze me," he said to Reb Yeshaye. "Here you are, living so lavishly, yet you still know how to learn."

288

During the years Reb Elimelech and Reb Zushe lived as wandering mendicants, every time they walked to Ludmir they would stay at the inn of a certain Hasid named Reb Aharon. They did this many times.

After they became famous, they traveled to Ludmir in a coach led by a pair of horses. The richest man in town heard that the two saintly brothers were coming. He went out to the nearest village to greet them and pleaded with them to grant him the great merit of hosting them. He would hand over his entire house to them and make sure that they were well fed and taken care of. The brothers neither agreed nor refused. They told him to return to town, where they would later arrive.

When they came to Ludmir, the brothers went to the home of Reb Aharon, where they usually stayed. The rich man rushed up, complaining, "What's going on? I've got everything prepared for you."

"Here's the deal," answered one of the brothers. "We're the same people we've always been, so we need to stay at our usual inn. You think we're more important now just because we're riding in a coach with a pair of horses. So how about the coach and horses stay with you?"

290

As a young man, Reb Mordche of Lekhevitsh was terribly poor. He and his entire family often went hungry. They didn't have a crust of bread to their name.

A relative once came to visit them. His wife poured out her heart to the visitor. She was at her wit's end; she didn't know what to do but couldn't stand seeing her children wasting away any longer. She burst out weeping.

The relative went to see Reb Mordche in his private room. He saw Reb Mordche lost in holy contemplation, humming a tune.

"Go see your family!" he said to Reb Mordche. "Your wife and children are crying, and you're singing?"

"They have good reason to cry," said Reb Mordche, "because they're depending on me, and I'm just flesh and blood, dust and ashes. But I depend on the Master of the Universe, who can do anything. So I sing..."

291

Reb Zundl Salanter was once riding from one town to the next in a wagon driven by a Jewish coachman. As they passed a field of cut hay, the coachman said to Reb Zundl, "You keep a lookout, make sure nobody sees me while I go grab a bit of hay for the horse."

Reb Zundl said nothing.

The coachman got down, went over to a haystack, seized an armful and started back to the wagon.

Reb Zundl started shouting, "They see you! They see you!"

The coachman got frightened, threw away the hay, jumped into the wagon, and drove on.

As he rode, he looked around—there was no one there.

"A fine thing, tricking a fellow Jew like that," he complained to Reb Zundl.

"God forbid!" said Reb Zundl. "Absolutely you were seen!"

"Who saw me?" wondered the coachman. "There isn't a soul around."

"From up above," Reb Zundl said, pointing his finger heavenward, "they saw you."

292

Reb Zundl Salanter had two sons-in-law, both great luminaries: Reb Shmuel Salant, who was the rabbi of Jerusalem for 70 years, and Reb Note Notkin, a leading member of the Jewish community of Jerusalem.

Now, just how a poor man like Reb Zundl acquired such wonderful sons-in-law is its own story:

When they began discussing possible matches for Reb Zundl's eldest daughter, Reb Shmuel Salant was already known throughout the region as a prodigy. They were thinking of marrying him off to a daughter of a rich man from Kovno, that kind of match. But Reb Zundl wanted Reb Shmuel to be his son-in-law, and he refused any other match for his daughter. He insisted that he already had a groom for his daughter—Reb Shmuel. Everyone smiled at his naiveté.

Reb Shmuel's father happened to pay a visit to Salant and heard about Reb Zundl's prediction that Reb Shmuel would be his son-in-law. Reb Shmuel's father was a fervently pious Jew. He agreed to the match, and they were married.

Here's what happened with the other son-in-law, Reb Note. It was hard to find a match for Reb Zundl's other daughter. Reb Zundl was already living in Jerusalem, and his daughter was old enough to marry but hadn't found a match. Reb Zundl swore that the first young man who arrived in Jerusalem as part of the first expedition from his home region, Lithuania, would be his son-in-law.

And one day a party arrived from Lithuania. As was the custom, the Jews of Jerusalem went to Motza, at the outskirts of the city, to greet the new arrivals from overseas. Reb Zundl spotted a young man dressed like a simple artisan. He approached and asked him, "Where are you from in Lithuania?"

"What difference does it make?" answered the youngster.

"Did you study in a yeshiva?" Reb Zundl asked further.

"Whose business is it?" the boy retorted.

Every question Reb Zundl asked him, he refused to answer.

"Would you like to be my son-in-law?" Reb Zundl asked.

"Yes," the boy answered.

The match went through. The terms were agreed on, and a date was set for the wedding.

But Reb Zundl was possessed with regret: had he been overbold and ended up with an ignoramus?

And the young man still refused to say who he was.

A few days later, Reb Zundl's son-in-law Reb Shmuel Salant was sitting with other scholars discussing Torah. The groom came in and listened for a few minutes, and then he commented, "My grandfather, the Shages Aryeh, sees it differently." And he repeated a passage from the *Shages Aryeh* by heart.

Reb Shmuel immediately rushed out to tell his father-in-law, Reb Zundl, who his new prospective son-in-law was, and the wedding was conducted with great joy.

294

When Reb Chaim Leyb Stavisker was seriously ill, they summoned a professor from Warsaw to see him. The professor came, examined the patient, and informed the rest of the household in another room that there was no hope. You can imagine the reaction. Reb Chaim Leyb asked what the professor had said, and they didn't tell him. But he could tell from their faces.

"What are you so worried about?" he told them. "So what if the professor says I won't make it? The Talmud interprets the verse, '*rapo yerape,* he will surely heal' to mean that doctors have permission to heal. But that only gives him permission to *heal*. Who gave him the authority to say who will live and who will die?"

295

Reb Yisroel, the Kozhenitser Maggid, was once told about an old, childless couple who were finally blessed with a boy, without going to a wonderworker for heavenly intercession.

"God has acted very sensibly," smiled the Kozhenitser. "Most people either come to see the Chozeh ["Seer"] of Lublin or me. This time God showed that He can provide a child all by Himself."

299

A cattle dealer came to see Reb Meirl Pshemishlaner to ask whether he should take his cattle to the market in Vienna.

"This week's Torah portion is Nitzavim, 'you are standing,'" said Reb Meirl. "That means you should stay where you are. Next week is Vayelekh, 'and he went,' so that's when you should go to the market."

The dealer followed his advice. The following week, the price for cattle crashed, and the merchant was impoverished.

He came to Reb Meirl complaining, "Rebbe, how could you? I lost my shirt following your advice!"

"What does he want from Meir?" shrugged the Rebbe. "Neither Meir nor his father's fathers ever dealt in cattle."

301

A young man once came to Reb Yisroel Itshe Rizhiner to receive rabbinic ordination. The Rizhiner was standing by the window, gazing into the courtyard. It was winter and the courtyard was entirely covered with snow. The young man came up and stood next to the Rizhiner, and he began to boast ad nauseum of his own righteousness and asceticism: he went about clad only in white; no drink passed through his lips other than plain, cold water; he placed nails in his shoes to suffer trials of pain; he would go out in the coldest weather to chafe his limbs in the freezing snow; and the local synagogue beadle would give him 40 lashes a day.

As the young man was speaking, a white horse wandered into the courtyard, walked up to the well, took a drink out of a pail, and then dove into the snow and began frisking around in it, the way horses do.

"Look," said the Rizhiner to the young man, "this creature right here also goes around in white; doesn't drink anything except water; has nails in his shoes; rolls around in the snow; and receives over 40 lashes from his master every day—yet after all that, he's still just a horse."

302

Reb Yisroel Rizhiner, as everyone knows, enjoyed a lavish lifestyle. He would ride around in his own coach like royalty.

A modern Jew once came to see him. He was struck by the luxury of the Rizhiner court. He asked the Rizhiner, "Tell me, Rebbe, why is it that old-time rebbes lived on almost nothing, dwelled in wooden huts, dressed themselves in plain linen, and went everywhere on foot, while today's rebbes live in proper palaces, wear velvet and satin, and travel in coaches?"

"Let me explain," responded the Rizhiner. "There are three types of people who come to see rebbes: Hasidim, ordinary householders, and impious troublemakers. All three give contributions, which the rebbe spends according to the nature of the donors. The money a Hasid gives, the rebbe spends on fulfilling commandments—tsitsis, tefillin, an esrog, or charity. The money a householder gives, he spends on his material needs and the needs of his family. The money the impious troublemakers give him, he spends on luxuries—horses, coaches, that sort of thing. In the old days when everyone was pious, the rebbes didn't have money to buy horses, so they had to walk. These days there are plenty of troublemakers, so the rebbes have money for all these luxuries."

305

One time, when Reb Naftoli Ropshitser was a young man and was staying in Lublin at the court of the Chozeh he went to the Chozeh and said, "Yesterday I had a vision of the Sheloh."

The Chozeh was impressed. "Really, a vision of the Sheloh? The author of the great kabbalistic work, the *Shney Luchos Habris*? Do you know, my child, that a vision of a wonderworker is on a higher level than a vision of the Prophet Elijah?" And as he said this, the Chozeh felt a little downcast: The holy Sheloh had visited his home to reveal himself to the Chozeh's student, but not to the Chozeh himself.

"I had the impression that the Sheloh was somehow angry at me, because he stood with his spine straight, facing the other way."

"Where was he standing?" asked the Chozeh.

"In the Rebbe's bookcase. He's still there now," answered Reb Naftoli, pointing to the two volumes of *Sheloh*, standing on the shelf among the other books.

307

Reb Azriel, the Rabbi of Lublin known as "the Iron Head," was a bitter opponent of Hasidism. When the Chozeh of Lublin died, Reb Azriel told the leader of the burial society not to provide a plot in the cemetery for the Chozeh—an insult and a disgrace. The local Hasidim decided to send Reb Naftoli Ropshitser, who was known for his shrewd mind, to persuade Reb Azriel to relent. Reb Naftoli went to see the rabbi and pleaded with him, "How could this be? How could you refuse him any kind of plot at all? At least let us bury him in one of the less important areas of the cemetery."

He managed to get the rabbi to agree that the burial could take place in one of the less desirable rows.

Reb Naftoli and the head of the burial society went to the cemetery to look for a plot. But earlier, he had gone and bribed the gravediggers, arranging that at his signal, they should immediately start digging. It was a dark and rainy night. Reb Naftoli and the gravediggers went from row to row. Reb Naftoli kept saying, "What's the difference? Here, there—anywhere." When they arrived at a row that Reb Naftoli liked, he casually commented, "As far as I'm concerned, it's fine."

The head of the burial society didn't say anything. Reb Naftoli signaled the gravediggers, and they immediately began digging. A bit later the head of the burial society realized that it was a very exalted row. He began protesting that he wasn't permitted to authorize burial in that row. But the deed was already done. Reb Azriel ruled that once the grave was dug it could not be changed.

310

Reb Naftoli Ropshitser used to say, "All the wonderworkers ask anyone who needs a miracle to come to them, and the wonderworkers will pray for them. I get up very early and ask God that everyone who needs a miracle should receive it right there at home, and they shouldn't come to me and think that it was I who helped them."

311

One of Reb Naftoli Ropshitser's Hasidim, a simpleton, once noticed the rebbe cutting his nails after he came out of the mikveh.

"Rebbe," the Hasid asked, "what is the kabbalistic reason why the Rebbe cuts his nails after he goes to the mikveh?"

Reb Naftoli made a serious face and answered like a proper rebbe, "This matter, my child, involves a deep secret. Only to a chosen few may it be revealed."

"Rebbe, what must one do in order to merit knowing the secret?" the Hasid humbly asked.

"It is a difficult undertaking," Reb Naftoli continued. "You have to fast 70 times, equal to the numerical values of the Hebrew word *sod*, 'secret,' and you have to immerse yourself in the mikveh 310 times."

"Rebbe, I swear I will do this," the Hasid answered enthusiastically. "Whatever it takes to be worthy of learning the great secret."

A long time later, the Hasid came to Reb Naftoli, "Rebbe, I did exactly what the Rebbe told me to do."

"Now I will reveal the secret to you," Reb Naftoli said in a friendly tone.

The Hasid closed his eyes and stood there with great reverence and care, ready to learn the deep secret from the rebbe.

"Now you will know," smiled the Rebbe, "that after the mikveh, the nails are softer, so they're easier to cut."

312

A sinner once came to Reb Naftoli to seek penance. He was ashamed to say that he was the sinner, so he claimed that a good friend of his, who was too ashamed to come see the Rebbe, had sent him. He enumerated his "friend's" many sins.

"What a fool your friend is!" smiled Reb Naftoli. "He could have just come himself and claimed that his 'friend' sent him."

318

Reb Chaim Sanzer once asked a disciple who was sitting at his table whether the servers had provided him with a portion of food.

"Rebbe," answered the disciple, full of piety, "I did not come here to eat."

"Sure," smiled Reb Chaim, "the soul likewise does not come to the world to eat. Yet all the same, if you don't give it any food, it runs off…"

320

Reb Chaim Sanzer once caught a cold and had a bad cough. He was told to drink tea for the cough.

During the third meal of that Shabbos, he was lost in religious fervor and extended his celebrations until late at night. His son, Reb Boruch, who was watchful of his father's health, ordered tea to be served. Reb Chaim was caught up in a state of religious ecstasy, transcendent from the world of material concerns, and didn't touch his tea. Reb Boruch reminded him a couple of times but Reb Chaim paid no notice. Finally, Reb Chaim became annoyed.

"What do you want from me?" he said to Reb Boruch. "In the spiritual realm, no one drinks tea."

"Yes, Papa," smiled Reb Boruch, "but in the spiritual realm, no one coughs, either."

321

One time, Reb Chaim Sanzer was standing by his window, looking outside. A disciple of his walked by. He knocked on the window and called the disciple inside.

"What would you do," Reb Chaim asked him, "if you were to find a purse full of gold coins?"

The disciple answered, "I would immediately give it away."

"You're a fool," Reb Chaim told him.

He called in a second disciple and asked him the same question.

"What am I, a fool?" answered the second disciple. "Obviously I would take it."

"You're a scoundrel," Reb Chaim told him, and ordered him to leave.

He called inside a third and asked him the same question.

"Rebbe," the third disciple said, "first, let me find it."

"You're a sage," Reb Chaim told him.

322

In his final years, Reb Chaim Sanzer selected Reb Aren, his younger son, as his successor rather than his elder son. The public was astonished.

"Let me tell you a story," said Reb Chaim.

> In a city, there once was a blind beggar. He sat in the market and begged.
>
> Everyone who passed by had pity on him and gave him alms. Some would give quite generously. In this way, the beggar was able to collect an enormous sum of money, and he bought himself houses and a variety of possessions. In short, he became a wealthy man.
>
> The beggar had several children, all healthy except for one who was blind. Before his death, he

bequeathed all of his possessions to his healthy children. To the blind son, he left nothing.

So people asked him, "What are you doing? Why are you passing over the blind son for his inheritance? On the contrary, you ought to give him more because he is blind, the poor thing."

"Think of it this way," answered the beggar. "My blind son will soon be rich like me: the public will take pity on him. But who will spare a thought for my healthy children?"

325

Reb Elye Guttmacher was a rabbi in Grayditz, a town in Prussia. He was well-known as a kabbalist and wonderworker, and he maintained the customs of a Hasidic rebbe, conducting festive meals, distributing remainders of his food to his followers, and accepting requests for intervention in Heaven on their behalf.

One time, a Hasidic Jew came from Poland to Grayditz on business and went to see the rabbi. He saw a rebbe surrounded by a crowd of Hasidim, just like in Poland. He was amazed: a rebbe in Prussia! He sat at the table, heard Torah, snatched leftovers, sang hymns, and couldn't get over the fact that this was happening in Prussia.

When he returned home to Poland, he went to his own rebbe and related that while he had been in Prussia, he had met a "good Jew," a Hasidic rebbe.

"A 'good Jew' in Prussia?" marveled the rebbe.

"Yes, Rebbe," answered the Hasid, "a good Jew, a tzaddik, a rebbe."

"A real rebbe with a beard and peyes?" the rebbe wondered further.

"Yes, a long beard, with long peyes, with a shtreiml."

"A shtreiml? In Prussia?"

"Yes, in Prussia."

"And what about fear of Heaven? Does he pray every day?"

"Does he pray? With preparatory recitations, after going to the mikveh—he prays until midday."

"And how does he pray? Nusach Ashkenaz?"

"God forbid! Nusach Sefarad, following the Ari."

"And people come to see him?"

"What a question! A crowd of Jews, may they be well, on a regular Shabbos more than twenty of them around the table."

"That many? And he conducts a tish?"

"Yes, and it lasts for hours."

"And they sing hymns?"

"Delightful melodies, with passion and intensity."

"And he delivers Torah insights?"

"Indeed! Zohar, Kabbalah, mysteries."

"Zohar, mysteries—in Prussia?" The rebbe couldn't get over it.

"Yes, in Prussia," repeated the Hasid.

"And he distributes leftovers?"

"Yes."

"And you got some?"

"Yes, but... only fish."

"Why only fish?" asked the rebbe.

"I mean...to take meat," stammered the Hasid, "somehow I didn't dare... I couldn't make myself do it. I don't know—after all, it's still Prussia."

327

During the great dispute over Maimonides, when his opponents spread the slander that he didn't behave according to the Torah, the sages of France traveled to see Maimonides in Egypt, to see for themselves how he conducted himself at home.

Maimonides understood why they had come. But he greeted them warmly, invited them to his home, sat them down, and showed them the greatest respect.

When they had sat down, Maimonides said to his servant, "Peter, serve wine to the guests."

The French sages looked at each other: How could Maimonides let a Gentile handle wine for Jews? It's clearly forbidden. "We're tired from our journey," they claimed as an excuse. "We'd rather drink water."

Some time later, Maimonides said to his servant, "Peter, kill the calf and cook it up for our guests."

The French sages couldn't believe what they were hearing. No ritual slaughter? The calf wouldn't be kosher. It seemed all the rumors were true.

"Since we're exhausted," they said to Maimonides, "we'd rather not eat meat."

So they had a bit of something else to eat and went to bed.

As they were settling down to sleep, they overheard Maimonides saying to the servant, "Peter, tomorrow morning, wake up early, find a person, cut him up into little pieces and prepare him for our guests."

The French sages were terrified. They didn't sleep a wink that night, waiting for daybreak. At first light, they got up and immediately began gathering their things to depart.

"What are you rushing for?" Maimonides asked them. "Stay awhile."

They told him the truth. They had heard and seen things that they never would have believed.

"Let me explain what you heard," smiled Maimonides. "My servant Peter isn't a Gentile but a learned Jew. The calf I told him to kill was a fetus, so it may be killed without kosher slaughter. The 'person' that I ordered him to cut up and cook is a vegetable that has that name because it's shaped like a person."

The French sages stayed with Maimonides for several days, delighted in discussing matters of Torah and scientific knowledge with him, and couldn't stop exclaiming over his wisdom and piety.

329

The Vilna Gaon, as everybody knows, almost never left his home. He sat in his room with the windows closed and shuttered, even when the sun was out. Day and night he studied and prayed.

In those years, the Dubner Maggid was famous for his parables and for his talented remonstrations against sin. His sermons and parables aroused Jewish hearts to repent and to fear God. Even confirmed sinners returned to a righteous path.

The Gaon wrote to the Maggid, asking him to come and rebuke the Gaon.

When the Dubner Maggid arrived, he saw that the Gaon lived in solitude and never stepped out of the house.

When the two were in private, the Dubner Maggid said, "It's not such a great feat to be the Vilna Gaon when you sit here all alone, fenced off from the world, and don't do anything except study Torah. If you went out among people, dealt with everyday matters, did commerce, and still remained the Vilna Gaon—now that would be some trick!"

The Gaon listened until the Maggid was finished and answered drily, "I don't do tricks."

330

In Vilna, they used to tell the following story about Reb Shoyelke, a self-confident rabbi who was appointed to rule on everyday questions of rabbinic law. In his younger days, he was a contemporary of the Vilna Gaon, Reb Elye.

One of Reb Elye's neighbors was a poor tailor. One Friday night, while the tailor sat at the table with his family and his two workers, singing and waiting for his wife to bring out the Shabbos tsimmes, something forbidden happened with the oven and it wasn't clear whether they were permitted to still eat the tsimmes.

The tailor sent one of his workers to ask the rabbi, Reb Shoyelke.

They waited for quite a while, but the worker hadn't returned. They couldn't stand to wait any longer.

The tailor's wife recalled that in the next courtyard over lived Reb Elye, who could also give a ruling. So they sent the other worker to ask Reb Elye.

Some time later, the first worker came back with an answer: "The rabbi says: kosher!"

The tailor was just about to have the tsimmes brought to the table when the other worker came in with an answer as well: "Reb Elye says it's not kosher."

Everyone was confused. What should they do? Who should they follow?

The tailor put on his coat, went to Reb Shoyelke and told him the story. "Go home," Reb Shoyelke said. "Soon Reb Elye and I will be coming over to taste your tsimmes."

The tailor ran home and when he'd regained his breath, announced, "The rabbi and Reb Elye are coming here to taste the tsimmes!"

The house was in an uproar—these were no everyday guests! The whole street found out that Reb Shoyelke and Reb Elye were coming to visit the tailor. They packed themselves into the tailor's apartment like sardines.

Reb Shoyelke went to the Gaon and said to him, "Come, Reb Elye, let's taste that tailor's nice, kosher tsimmes."

"If you tell me to," answered the Gaon, "I'll eat it. You're the authority here."

A short time later, the rabbi and the Gaon arrived at the tailor's house. Everyone moved back to let them through and stood there, waiting to see what would happen.

The rabbi and the Gaon sat down at the table and Reb Shoyelke ordered the tsimmes brought in.

The tailor's wife ladled some of the tsimmes into a brand-new serving dish. With trembling hands, she brought it to the table.

As she passed under the chandelier, a candle suddenly fell right into the serving dish.

The crowd was struck with fear.

Reb Shoyelke stood up and said to the Gaon, "Heaven has shown us that you are right."

332

During the dispute between Reb Boruch Mezhbuzher, the Ba'al Shem Tov's grandson, and Reb Shneur Zalmen of Liadi, Reb Boruch accused Reb Shneur Zalmen: "They say that while you were imprisoned in St. Petersburg, you discussed Kabbalah with a Gentile. Is that true?"

"True," answered Reb Shneur Zalmen, "but that Gentile knows Kabbalah better than some respected rabbis I may know."

335

The Rabbi of Lublin, Reb Azriel, known as "the Iron Head," bitterly opposed Hasidism.

When Reb Yankev Yitschok, the Chozeh of Lublin, revealed his holiness to the world and people began to travel to see him, Reb Azriel protested vigorously. Time and again, he complained to the Chozeh that the latter had no right to act like a rebbe when he himself knew that he was just an ordinary Jew.

One time the Chozeh responded, "What should I do? Everybody comes to see me."

"I have an idea," said Reb Azriel. "When people come to see you, tell them the truth—that you're a simple Jew. They won't come anymore."

The Chozeh did just that. The next Shabbos, when everyone was gathered around the table, the Chozeh stood up and said, with tears in his eyes, "Gentlemen, you should know that I'm just an ordinary Jew. I am neither learned nor pious, and you have nothing to learn from me."

The Hasidim were so deeply moved by the rebbe's humility that it drew them even closer to him.

A few days later Reb Azriel met the Chozeh, and asked, "So did you follow my advice?"

"Yes," answered the Chozeh, "but it didn't help. On the contrary, the crowd took it for saintly modesty, and now they're even more devoted to me."

"If that's the case," said Reb Azriel, "I have a different piece of advice. Tell them that you are a genius and a saint, and they'll think you're arrogant and they'll abandon you."

"Never!" said the Chozeh. "I may be no rebbe, but I'm no liar, either."

336

Reb Yisroel Rizhiner had the ascetic practice of eating as simply and modestly as possible. Reb Avrom Heshl, the rabbi of Apt, served lavish meals with various dishes and drinks and ate and drank as much as his heart desired.

The Rizhiner once came to visit the Apter. The Apter enthusiastically greeted him and ordered fine refreshments befitting such an honored guest.

But when they sat down at the table, the Apter barely ate.

"Why are you eating so little?" asked the Rizhiner. "That's not like you."

Reb Avrom Heshl answered, "You know that Shabbos is the guest of the weekdays. So the weekdays honor Shabbos with rich foods, meat, fish, and tasty treats. Holidays are the guest of Shabbos. When a holiday falls on Shabbos, Shabbos honors that guest with an extra dish. But when the holiday guest is someone who doesn't eat—for example, the holy fast of Yom Kippur—Shabbos doesn't eat then either."

339

Reb Akiva Eiger and Reb Yankev of Lissa once came to Warsaw to participate in a rabbinical assembly. Of course, all of Warsaw turned out to greet the two great rabbis. When they climbed into their coach, the crowd unhitched the horses and pulled the wagon themselves to honor these two luminaries.

When Reb Akiva Eiger saw this, he thought that they were doing it to honor Reb Yankev of Lissa. So without a word, he got down and joined the crowd pulling the coach. It was so packed that no one noticed him. Meanwhile Reb Yankev, who was looking out the other side, thought that this was all in honor of Reb Akiva, so he got down to help. And for a little while the whole Jewish community of Warsaw pulled the wagon like that before anyone noticed it was completely empty.

341

During Reb Akiva Eiger and Reb Yankev of Lissa's trip to Warsaw, they went on Shabbos to pray in the same study house. Naturally they were received with great honor and given seats at the very front by the Eastern wall, as befits such leading luminaries.

When the time came to distribute the honors for the Torah reading, the gabbai was flummoxed. There was only one shlishi, but two great rabbis. Who should get it? After long discussions, it was decided that Reb Akiva Eiger would get shlishi, and Reb Yankev of Lissa would get shishi, the next most desirable.

As they returned to their inn after the services, Reb Yankev saw that Rabbi Akiva was upset. He understood that Reb Akiva was distressed at having been given the greater honor.

"Don't worry, Reb Akiva, you didn't get shlishi because you're a greater scholar than I. It's only that you have more Jews in Posen than I do in Lissa."

Reb Akiva Eiger was immediately put at ease.

344

Reb Moyshe Sofer, the "Chasam Sofer," once sat talking with Reb Mordche Benet, the rabbi of Nikolsburg. As they were talking, he mentioned that he had once reminded Reb Mordche Benet of a certain passage in the Jerusalem Talmud which the latter had forgotten.

Realizing that this might sound like an insult, he immediately caught himself. "But of course, a large wagon loaded up with many precious goods has to take the highway right into the marketplace and can't get through on a side street or back alley. But an empty, little wagon can take the side streets or squeeze through a back alley. It's the same with the Rabbi of Nikolsburg and me. The Rabbi of Nikolsburg is full of Torah, Talmud, and codes of law—naturally he can't remember an incidental remark thrown in somewhere in the Jerusalem Talmud. But I don't carry that much around in my head, so I'm able to remember a side remark."

345

Reb Lipe Mirer tended to rule very leniently on civil and religious matters. On the other hand Reb Yeruchem Leyb, the Gadol of Minsk, was very stringent.

They once met. Naturally, they discussed Torah, particularly practical, everyday legal questions. During the conversation, the Gadol of Minsk asked Reb Lipe why he was so lenient.

"I'll tell you," answered Reb Lipe. "Since I tend to rule leniently, if I God forbid were to make a mistake, it would be to declare something kosher that's actually forbidden. And one day—may it not be for a hundred years—Jews would summon me to the Heavenly Court for feeding them nonkosher food. But with your stringencies, you risk declaring kosher food forbidden. After you pass away—may it not be for a hundred years—you'd be summoned to the Heavenly Court by an ox. He will complain that you declared him forbidden and took away his chance to become holy, that Jews might eat him with a blessing."

346

Reb Mordche of Lekhevitsh once went to see Reb Avremele Trisker. They discussed Hasidism, and the various worship styles of the great tsaddikim.

Reb Avremele asked Reb Mordche: "Did your teachers leave behind any books?"

"Yes," answered Reb Mordche.

"Printed or in manuscript?"

"Neither," answered Reb Mordche. "In Jewish hearts."

347

Reb Ayzl Chaver, the rabbi of Suvalk, had a dispute with Reb Chaim Vistinitser. He sent his son to Reb Leybele Kovner to convince him to pronounce a ban on Reb Chaim. Reb Leybele received Reb Ayzl's son as an honored guest, and he asked his wife to prepare a holiday meal with fish, chicken, and wine.

"We have an important guest," he said, "a son of Reb Ayzl."

As they sat at the table, Reb Leybele talked to Reb Ayzl's son about his father. During the fish course he asked, "Does your father eat fish?"

"Yes," answered Reb Ayzl's son.

With the chicken: "Does your father eat chicken?"

"Yes."

And it was the same with every course.

"And Reb Chaim," concluded Reb Leybele before he began to recite the prayer after meals, "eats nothing but bread and water. So tell your father that what he eats in one day, Reb Chaim doesn't eat in a whole month, and what Reb Chaim learns in one day, your father doesn't learn in a whole month."

348

Before Reb Avreml became the first Slonimer rebbe, he was a trusted companion of Reb Ayzl Kharif's. They would often sit and discuss both Torah and current affairs. Reb Ayzl, who had no patience for fools and fiercely opposed the Hasidic movement, greatly respected Reb Avreml's scholarship, and they became fast friends.

When Reb Avreml became a Hasidic rebbe, however, it was as if they suddenly lived in different worlds.

A little while after becoming rebbe, Reb Avreml went to see Reb Ayzl.

"Avreml," Reb Ayzl asked, "*you*—a rebbe?"

"Jews made me a rebbe," answered Reb Avreml in typical Hasidic fashion.

"And that makes you a holy saint, all of a sudden?" asked Reb Ayzl.

"That's the power of Jews," answered Reb Avreml. "When they unite around one man and start coming to his court, they draw holiness onto him. It's like trumah, the portion of the crop tithed for the Temple. It's only simple grain, but as soon as a Jew designates it as trumah, it becomes holy."

"You only just became a rebbe and already you've forgotten your learning," retorted Reb Ayzl. "The Mishnah states clearly: Trumah designated by an imbecile is no trumah at all."

350

Reb Yoshe Ber spent one summer in the countryside at Novominsk. The Novominsker Rebbe came to visit him. Reb Yoshe Ber greeted him warmly, invited him to sit down, and offered tea. Before the rebbe made a blessing on the tea, he swayed back and forth, sighed, and gazed in deep concentration, as Hasidic rebbes often do.

When he finally finished the blessing and took a drink, Reb Yoshe Ber innocently commented, "Pretty bad case of hiccups, huh?"

352

For a while Reb Hersh Leyb and Reb Yoshe Ber were coheads of the yeshiva in Volozhin. As often happens in that situation, conflicts developed between them, and the two didn't get along. In any case, they had very different personalities. Reb Hersh Leyb was straightforward and simple. Reb Yoshe Ber was complex and brilliant.

They were once both at a wedding. The feast put Reb Yoshe Ber in a lighthearted mood. He decided to have some fun with Reb Hersh Leyb.

"Gentlemen!" he announced. "I'll show you a trick. Place nuts at all four corners of the table, and put a plate in the middle. All I will do is say a few simple words, and abracadabra, all the nuts will be on the plate!"

"You're playing pranks," Reb Hersh Leyb called out. "What are you, a Hasidic rebbe or a magician?"

"I'll bet you three rubles," said Reb Yoshe Ber. "Agreed?"

"Agreed!" answered Reb Hersh Leyb.

They placed nuts at the four corners of the table and set a plate in the middle. The whole crowd stared expectantly at Reb Yoshe Ber. He waited a while, looking back at the crowd. Then he said to his assistant, "Yankl, take the nuts and put them on the plate."

The assistant did just that. Everyone laughed.

"Pay up," said Reb Yoshe Ber to Reb Hersh Leyb. "I won!"

"But you deceived me," complained Reb Hersh Leyb. "That wasn't the bet. What kind of trick is it, getting your own assistant to put the nuts onto the plate?"

But Reb Yoshe Ber wouldn't back down. "You know what?" he proposed. "Let's put the question to the rabbis who are sitting here at the wedding table."

The rabbis heard both sides, talked it over, and ruled that it was really a deception. But that in itself is a trick, which was exactly what Reb Yoshe Ber had promised. So Reb Hersh Leyb had to pay.

"You're wrong, gentlemen," smiled Reb Yoshe Ber. "My opponent is right. It's no great trick to fool Reb Hersh Leyb."

354

Reb Yoshe Ber Brisker and Reb Yankev Dovid Slutsker once rode in the same carriage. Naturally, they discussed Torah. They fell into an argument. Reb Yankev Dovid got out of the carriage and sat down next to the coachman.

And that's how they came to town.

The townspeople were puzzled to see two rabbis, one riding inside and one on the coachman's seat.

They greeted the one sitting next to the coachman: "*Sholem aleykhem*, Rebbe! Where are you from? And who's the rabbi sitting inside?"

Reb Yankev Dovid answered, "I'm Reb Yoshe Ber of Brisk, and the one sitting inside is Reb Yankev Dovid of Slutsk. It's beneath Reb

Yankev Dovid's honor to have me sitting next to him, so I'm sitting next to the coachman."

"Don't believe him!" Reb Yoshe Ber stuck his head out the window and shouted. "I'm Yoshe Ber. *He's* Reb Yankev Dovid."

"Rebbe," said Reb Yankev Dovid, "it won't help. Everyone knows how humble you are..."

355

Reb Yisroel Salanter once traveled to Kelm. He immediately went to visit Reb Leybele Chosid. Reb Leybele didn't recognize Reb Yisroel. He greeted him warmly, as he would any person he met, but he was in a great hurry.

"Where are you rushing to, Rebbe?" asked Reb Yisroel.

"I'm on my way to greet a distinguished visitor," answered Reb Leybele. "A great man of our people, the genius of our generation, a saint upon whose merits rests the world."

"Who is he?" asked Reb Yisroel.

"Reb Yisroel Salanter," answered Reb Leybele.

"*That* one you call 'a genius, a saint'?" Reb Yisroel asked skeptically.

"Don't talk like that," Reb Leybele pleaded. "I can't stand it."

356

Reb Shmuel Moliver was deeply engaged in the movement to settle the Land of Israel. He tried to convince the greatest rabbis of his time, especially Reb Yitschok Elchonon. Reb Yitschok Elchonon was the leading rabbinic authority of his generation, and his word was respected throughout the Jewish world. Reb Yitschok Elchonon believed in the Hovevei Zion movement, but those in his circle would not allow him to publicly declare his support. After great efforts on Reb Shmuel's part, Reb Yitschok Elchonon agreed to call a meeting in Kovno to discuss the settlement of the Land of Israel.

The day of the meeting, Reb Shmuel arrived in Kovno for the

meeting. He immediately went to pay his respects to Reb Yitschok Elchonon. Reb Yitschok Elchonon welcomed him with great honor and seated him at the head of the table. Then Reb Yitschok Elchonon explained that the meeting had to be postponed.

Reb Shmuel guessed who had gotten to Reb Yitschok Elchonon, but he said nothing. Before he left, Reb Yitschok Elchonon invited him to dinner. Reb Shmuel promised to come.

That evening, Reb Yitschok Elchonon's assistant came to the inn where Reb Shmuel was staying to bring him to the rabbi's home. On their way there, Reb Shmuel suddenly stopped, excused himself for a minute, and hurried back to the inn.

When he returned, the assistant asked him, "Rebbe, why did you go back?"

"I went back," smiled Reb Shmuel, "to tell the innkeeper to make supper for me. Who knows? Your rebbe might change his mind, and I'd be left without any supper!"

359

Once, when the Jewish painter Jozef Israëls was working on his famous painting "A Son of the Ancient Race," the door opened, and a stranger walked in. The newcomer spoke no word of greeting. He walked a few steps closer, looked at the painting for a while, and began reciting Psalms, starting with the very first verse of the first chapter: "Happy is the man who did not walk in the counsel of the wicked, and stood not in the path of the sinners."

Israëls stared at him.

When the stranger had finished reciting the entire first chapter of Psalms, he approached Israëls, shook his hand and said, "I am Adolf Sonnenthal, of Vienna. Both of us are Jewish artists: you a painter, and I, of course, an actor! I came to acquaint myself with you, and couldn't think of a more appropriate way to do so than by way of a chapter of Psalms."

"Well, I like that approach very much," said Israëls. "So by all means, sit down and I will recite the second chapter."

And Israëls began: "Why do the peoples gather…"

But Sonnenthal interrupted him: "Please don't be offended, but declamation is *my* craft. I'll perform the second chapter, and you depict it in a painting."

Israëls agreed.

Sonnenthal declaimed the second chapter in his fine and strong voice, while Israëls painted a new picture.

It was in that picture, in his old age, that the painter found his Jewish soul. But he did not merit to live long enough to complete the picture.

361

Mendele Mocher Seforim bitterly opposed the cultural politics of Achad Ha'am. He didn't believe in the project of creating a spiritual center in the Land of Israel.

"If I were up to it," he said once, "I'd take Achad Ha'am and hang him up by his 'spirituality.' And then," he immediately added, "I'd eulogize him and weep bitter tears over our great loss."

368

Reb Ayzl Kharif once went to visit someone and found a copy of his book *Emek Yehoshua* bound together in one volume with Reb Yitschok Elchonon's *Nakhal Yitschok*. Reb Yitschok Elchonon's text came first in the volume.

"That's odd," smiled Reb Ayzl. "They say I'm the crazy one, but it's others they tie up first!"

372

Someone once asked Reb Yoshe Ber: "How is it, Rebbe, that many of the insights in your *Beis Levi* can be found in other books as well?"

"You need to understand," answered Reb Yoshe Ber. "If you're going the right way, you'll find a lot of other people going the same way. If you're going the wrong way, you'll be alone, and you won't meet anyone else."

374

A young man, a Maskil, once came to Reb Ayzik Meir Dik with an essay for which he sought Dik's approval.

"Young man," Dik said to him, "if you want to be a Jewish author, you have to take on the discipline of peddling your writings from home to home, and suffering poverty and deprivation until you turn 40."

"And once I'm 40?" eagerly asked the young man.

"By then," smiled Dik, "you'll have gotten used to it."

773

When Reb Chaim Volozhiner's son Reb Itsele was a young man, he planned to travel abroad to study secular subjects. Reb Chaim wouldn't permit it. Naturally, Reb Chaim wanted his son to become a great Talmud scholar.

As they laid the foundation for the new yeshiva he was building in Volozhin, Reb Chaim remarked, "With this, I am walling in my Itsele."

790

Reb Shayele Kutner, while still a boy, often came to Reb Zalmen Poyzner's estate. His father was the private tutor for Reb Zalmen's children, so Reb Shayele would come to visit his father. Reb Zalmen was known as a sharp scholar. Though Reb Shayele was still a boy, he was known as a genius. Reb Zalmen enjoyed discussing scholarly matters with the young Shayele.

Reb Zalmen's routine was to leave on Saturday night for Warsaw, where he conducted major business deals, spend the whole week there, and return home on Friday.

One Shabbos, Reb Zalmen expressed a novel insight. Little Shayele refuted it, Reb Zalmen defended it, and Shayele refuted it once again. They went back and forth until Reb Zalmen got stuck without a response.

Saturday night, Reb Zalmen set off for Warsaw. On the way, he realized that he was right, and there was no merit to Shayele's argument. He ordered the coachmen to turn around. Arriving home in the middle of the night, he found everyone asleep and the gate bolted. Reb Zalmen banged on the door. Everyone, including little Shayele, woke up. The household was panicked at Reb Zalmen's unexpected return.

"What happened?" everyone asked.

"On account of you, little one," Reb Zalmen said to Shayele, "I turned around. Your challenge simply doesn't hold water," and he began to explain his defense.

Little Shayele didn't let him go on for very long before quickly refuting his position. Reb Zalmen stood there, disappointed.

"I turned around for nothing," he sighed. "It wasn't worthwhile."

And in distress he rode off to Warsaw.

792

Before Reb Yechiel Michl Navarodker, the *Aruch Hashulchan*, became the town rabbi, he was a storekeeper, the owner of a textile shop in the marketplace. His wife minded the store while he studied all day and all night. The license for the store was in his name.

When the inspector would come to town to check up on licenses, Reb Yechiel Michl had to be in the store himself.

Once he was seen walking in the marketplace, searching among the stores.

"Reb Yechiel Michl," he was asked, "what are you looking for?"

"I'm looking for my store," he answered.

794

Reb Elye Chaim Lodzher devoted a great deal of time to the town's free community school. He supervised the lessons, made sure the poor children had food and clothing, and saw to it that they had a useful occupation upon leaving the school.

There once was a boy who studied there, an excellent student but a foundling, with no mother or father to watch over him. He stood out amongst his classmates as exceptionally bright. Reb Elye Chaim practically never let the child out of his sight, caring for him as if he were one of his own.

When the boy grew up and left the school, Reb Elye Chaim sent him off to a yeshiva. The young man studied diligently there and gained a reputation as a true prodigy.

Some years later, a wealthy Jew came into the yeshiva looking for a proper son-in-law, as was the practice in those days. The rosh yeshiva introduced him to the young man from Lodz, who made a good impression on the prospective father-in-law.

So the rich man inquired about his family. They confessed that no one knew the answer, since he was a foundling. The rich man decided the match was beneath him—he couldn't risk marrying into a bad family.

The rosh yeshiva told Reb Elye Chaim what had happened. Reb Elye Chaim wrote to the rich man that *he*, Reb Elye Chaim, the rabbi of Lodz, was now the young man's father. Now would that do?

The match was made, and Reb Elye Chaim performed the wedding ceremony. The erstwhile foundling devoted himself day and night to his studies and grew up to be an extraordinary scholar and Jew.

795

Reb Dovid Serdeler was famous throughout Hungary as a wit who came up with stinging sayings.

Once he was seen holding the *Pnei Yehoshua* in his hand, rocking it back and forth.

"Rebbe," they asked him, "what are you doing?"

"Oh, he babbles like a baby, the *Pnei Yehoshua*."

800

Near Apt, where Reb Avrom Yehoshua Heshl was the rabbi, there lived a Lithuanian scholar, an opponent of Hasidism. When the Apter Rabbi revealed himself to the world to be a holy saint and grew famous, the Lithuanian scholar went to Apt to see what the big deal was.

The morning after he arrived, he went to the synagogue. As he entered, he saw the Apter Rabbi sitting lost in thought and smoking his pipe. The Lithuanian scholar completed his prayers and then his course of daily study: a chapter of Mishnah, a folio of Gemara, a few points in the Shulchan Aruch. By then it was already midday, and here was the Apter Rabbi still sitting and smoking.

He approached the Apter and said, "What's going on, Rebbe? It's long past the set time for morning prayers."

"I'll tell you," answered the Apter. "You got up this morning and immediately started praying. After you prayed, you sat down to study. I got up and began to say the first words upon waking, 'I give thanks to You, living and enduring King, that you returned my soul to me...' but then I wondered: Who is this 'I' and who is this 'You?' I'm stuck there, and can't get any further."

803

One winter morning, Reb Pinches Koritser sat in his synagogue after services. He heard his Hasidim speaking of the Evil Inclination, which incites and seduces people with all its might, trying to trip them up and catch them in his net.

"The Evil Inclination isn't just a seducer, but a liar too," interjected Reb Pinches. "Listen to this strange piece of business he tried with me today.

"I woke up in the morning, and wanted to get up to go purify myself in the mikveh. I look up—the Evil Inclination is standing there.

"'How can you bathe when it's so cold?' he asked. 'It's bitter out there. The mikveh is frozen solid.'

"'You know what?' I said to him. 'You lie here, in this nice warm bed, and I'll go bathe.' I wanted to shake him off at least for a few minutes. And he agreed.

"I went to the mikveh, broke open the ice, and went in. And what do I see? The Evil Inclination standing right next to me in the water.

"He's a shameless liar. Don't believe him for a second."

812

Reb Aren Karliner used to say: "Anyone who's all Jew at home, is only half Jew on the road; and anyone who's half Jew at home—on the road, he is barely a quarter."

816

Reb Yankev Yitschok, the Chozeh of Lublin, used to say: "Better a wicked man who knows he's wicked than a saint who knows he's holy."

822

Once Reb Yisroel Salanter came to a spa. On the way, he met a rabbi traveling in the same railroad car. They introduced themselves, sat together, and chatted about Torah and current events.

As they were approaching a station, the rabbi pulled out of his pack some stale bread that he had brought from home, and he invited Reb Yisroel to share it with him. Reb Yisroel thanked him.

When they pulled into the station, Reb Yisroel got out and bought some fresh bread. The rabbi was amazed: Reb Yisroel Salanter eating Gentile bread?

"Don't be offended, Rebbe," the rabbi said. "How can it be that you eat bread from Gentile bakeries?"

"I'll tell you," answered Reb Yisroel. "I'm not the one paying for my trip to the spa. A good friend of mine is covering the costs. But he did so on the condition that I set aside all of the optional stringencies and take care of my health. So if I'm strict and avoid eating fresh bread on the way, I'll be keeping the stringency of avoiding Gentile bread. But I'll commit the sins of robbery and deceit."

830

A Jewish merchant once came to Reb Chaim Volozhiner and complained:

"Rebbe, I've run into a disaster! I sent lumber overseas to Prussia, but the border guards won't let it through. I'll be ruined."

"Don't worry," said Reb Chaim, "God will help you."

Meanwhile the price of wood rose, and the merchant earned thousands of rubles.

He happily came to see Reb Chaim and said, "Rebbe, now I see Heaven's special care."

Reb Chaim answered, "That's the difference between a rich man and a poor man. The poor man sees Heaven's workings every day, the rich man, only once in several years."

834

Reb Moyshe Sofer, the Chasam Sofer, used to say: "People frequently complain that they don't have enough to live on. But I've never heard anyone say that he didn't have enough to die on."

840

When Reb Moyshe Yachnes became a bar-mitzvah, his father took him to Reb Yisroel Ba'al Shem Tov for a blessing.

Reb Yisroel looked at the lad and said to him: "My child, if you want to have a long life, don't become famous."

841

Reb Yisroel Ba'al Shem Tov thought very highly of his disciple Reb Yankev Yoysef, the author of the *Toldos Yankev Yoysef.*

He frequently said: "Master of the Universe, you owe me a big *yasher-koyech*, for giving you such a Yosele."

843

A Jewish tax collector once came to see Reb Yankev Yoysef to ask for a blessing to earn a good living.

The Toldos glowered from under his bushy brows and simply said: "Repent."

"Ah," sighed the Jew, "it's a shame that our Rebbe isn't alive anymore."

"Why's that?" asked the Toldos.

"Once," the tax collector related, "someone brought me some stolen goods as a payment, and I accepted them. Sometime later the theft was discovered, and they began to investigate. I was afraid they'd find the stolen goods in my possession. So I went to see the Ba'al Shem Tov. I didn't tell him that I had the stolen goods, just that I was scared I'd be framed. The Rebbe told me to wait. When he came back from the bathhouse, he said:

"'Why did you tell me you were afraid you'd be framed? You're the one who's got the goods!'

"'So what should I do, Rebbe?'

"'Go home in peace. They won't find it in your possession.'

"Now," the tax collector concluded, "look at the difference between you and the Rebbe. The Rebbe knew I'd stolen and didn't tell me to repent. And you—I haven't yet stolen a thing, and already you're telling me to repent."

845

An unlearned Jew, a wealthy leaseholder, regularly traveled to see Reb Zushe Anipoler to give him a contribution so that the Rebbe would intercede in Heaven on his behalf.

One time the leaseholder came, but Reb Zushe wasn't home.

"Where's the Rebbe?" he asked.

"He went to see his own rebbe in Mezritsh," he was told.

"Is that so?" asked the leaseholder. "My Rebbe has his *own* rebbe? Uh, why don't I just go to *his* rebbe?"

The leaseholder went to the Maggid in Mezritsh and gave him a contribution.

It turned out to be a bad year for him and his fortunes began to decline.

His wife scolded him: "It's just what you deserve. Why did you abandon your old Rebbe?"

So the leaseholder went to see Reb Zushe, told him the whole story, and tried to puzzle it out: "As long as I came to see the Rebbe, I did fine. When I tried going to the Rebbe's rebbe, my luck ran out."

"You listen to me," said Reb Zushe. "As long as you were willing to give to whomever it may be—say, a Zushe—God was willing to give to whomever it may be—say, you. Once you started getting picky, then God started getting picky, too."

854

Reb Naftoli Ropshitser came from a prestigious family. All of his forebears were saints and scholars, both on his mother's side and his father's.

Once, when a large group of Hasidim were gathered around the table, Reb Naftoli recited his great lineage going back many generations, and concluded: "There's nobody in the world with ancestors like mine."

"Rebbe," a rich Hasid from Siebenbuergen said, "*My* ancestors are even more impressive."

This was news to Reb Naftoli. He called over the Jew from Siebenbuergen and asked him, "Who are your ancestors?"

"Rebbe," the Hasid responded, "I'm the only one in my entire family pious enough to put on tefillin every morning and wash before I eat."

"Well," Reb Natfoli smiled, "this guy from Siebenbuergen has a point!"

863

Reb Yisroel Pilever used to sit down with the congregation after morning services and drink to everyone's good health.

One time they noticed him removing his Rashi's tefillin as usual towards the end of the morning prayers, but he skipped switching into Rabbenu Tam's tefillin for the final part of the service, instead going over to the table and sitting down to have a drink with everyone. Everyone was astonished. They knowingly stroked their chins: must be a profound, mystical secret! Something beyond the ken of everyday Jews.

A beloved follower of Reb Yisroel's gathered up his courage and asked: "Rebbe, what is the spiritual purpose for the Rebbe (may he be well!) drinking l'chaim before putting on Rabbenu Tam's tefillin?"

"Ah," replied the Rebbe. "My purpose is simple. A couple of times now when I've waited until after—by then the schnapps was all gone."

885

Once, an author came to seek a letter of approbation for his book from Reb Ayzl Kharif. As usual, Reb Ayzl refused. But the author wouldn't take no for an answer. Reb Ayzl couldn't get rid of him.

Reb Ayzl took a piece of paper, wrote a handful of words of approval at the top, and signed at the very bottom of the page.

"Rebbe," asked the author, "why is your signature all the way at the bottom?"

"It's an explicit verse in the Torah," smiled Reb Ayzl. "'Keep far from a false matter.'"

892

Shmuel Yoysef Fuenn was a remarkable scholar who had written several books. For years, he edited *HaCarmel*, where he published hundreds of articles. On top of that, he was wealthy, owning a brickwork which supplied Vilna and the surrounding region.

Reb Ayzl Kharif of Slonim once said of him, "You can tell how good a brick factory is by how stiff the bricks are. And you can tell how good a writer is by how supple his language is. But Fuenn has it backwards: His bricks are soft and it's his Hebrew that's stiff."

895

Elazar Atlas was an incisive critic who was unafraid to take on anyone, big or small. In one of his articles about the Council of Four Lands, he boldly contradicted giants of Jewish history like Graetz, Dubnow, Harkavy, and others.

A friend of his once asked: "Tell me, Reb Elazar, why weren't you afraid to go up against such big shots?"

"You're surprised?" smiled Atlas. "I'll tell you a story:

> A nobleman was angry with the Jew who leased his estate. The Jew didn't have the money to pay the lease, or maybe he offended the nobleman in some other way. Who knows what would set off a nobleman in those days? The nobleman announced his sentence: He had to spend the night sleeping with a bear in its cage.
>
> When he heard this, the Jew practically fell dead on the spot. A bear! He fell at the nobleman's feet, pleading: "Dear master, have pity on me, on my

wife and child, and do not let me be slain by a wild beast."

The nobleman relented a bit and said, "Don't cry, Moshke, I've got some advice for you. You put on a bear costume, and creep into the cage on all fours. The bear will think you're one of his own and won't bother you."

So the Jew put on a bear's pelt, got down on all fours, crept into the cage all atremble, and plastered himself to the door. When he caught sight of the bear, he knew he was done for and shouted, "Shema Yisroel..."

The bear interrupted him and finished: "The Lord is One!"

He approached a little closer—the bear was just as Jewish as he was.

Living Together

379

Reb Avrom Abish, the rabbi of Frankfurt, was a world-class scholar and a righteous Jew. He regularly went around town collecting for the poor and needy, and for suffering Talmud scholars and descendants of good families.

Once during the month of Elul, he approached a merchant from out of town to ask for a contribution for the poor. The merchant didn't recognize the rabbi of Frankfurt and thought he was just another itinerant beggar. He was busy with his accounts and grumbled, "Go away, go away, I don't have any time!"

Reb Avrom Abish didn't say a word and went away.

When he had left, the merchant realized that his cane was missing. He had no doubt that this was the beggar's doing. He ran out into the street and chased him down, shouting: "Thief, give me back my cane! Just because I wouldn't give you any money, you have to steal my cane?"

"God forbid!" said Reb Avrom Abish. "I didn't steal your cane."

The merchant became furious and started beating him. Reb Avrom Abish accepted the blows and didn't say who he was.

On the Shabbos between Rosh Hashanah and Yom Kippur, the rabbi gave a sermon in the synagogue. The whole town went to hear him, the out-of-town merchant among them. When he arrived, the rabbi was already in the middle of his speech. The merchant pressed through the crowd closer to the Holy Ark so that he could hear better. When he got close enough that he could see who was standing on the platform, he fainted dead away. After he was revived and they took him out into the anteroom, he burst into tears. How could he have insulted and beaten Reb Avrom Abish, the rabbi of Frankfurt? Those surrounding him comforted him and suggested that when the rabbi finished his sermon, he should approach the rabbi and ask for forgiveness. A true saint like Reb Avrom Abish would certainly forgive him.

After the sermon, when everyone crowded around the rabbi to praise the sermon, the merchant also got close to him. But when Reb Avrom Abish saw him, he assumed that the man was still upset about his cane. He approached the merchant and began to try to appease him in front of the whole congregation, "Please don't be angry with me for causing you distress. Believe me, I don't know what to say. I'm declaring to you here, in this holy place, that I didn't take your cane!"

380

Once while Reb Chaim Volozhiner's brother Zalmele was sitting and studying in the study house in Vilna, a Jew came up to him carrying a volume of the Mishnah with the tractate "Dmay," which deals with produce sold by an ordinary Jew. The rabbis deemed that such unlearned Jews could not be trusted to properly tithe their produce on their own, leaving its status in doubt. The Jew told Reb Zalmele that he had a sharp commentary on "Dmay." In this Jew's Vilna dialect, the word for commentary, said by most as *peyresh*, came out as *peyres*, the same as the word for "produce."

Reb Zalmele listened to the commentary—it was utterly meaningless.

He mocked the Jew, saying, "It seems that your commentary is indeed *peyres dmay*," meaning here—the product of an ignoramus.

The man slunk away as though he'd been kicked.

After he went out, Reb Zalmele realized that he had humiliated the man. He ran out to ask forgiveness, but the man had already left. Reb Zalmele was deeply distressed. He waited impatiently for the next day, but that whole next day passed and the man didn't appear in the study hall. Reb Zalmele began making inquiries to see whether anyone knew him, where he lived... nobody knew. Reb Zalmele became even more upset and couldn't rest. Every day he went to a different street, a different study hall, hoping to find the man—but it was no use. He didn't see the man anywhere. Eventually Reb Zalmele became sick with anguish.

His father-in-law, Reb Michl Peseles, couldn't stand to see his son-in-law suffer. He had an idea. He arranged for one of his close friends, a clever fellow, to approach Reb Zalmele disguised as the humiliated man.

The fellow went into the study hall, approached Reb Zalmele, greeted him and said, "How are you, Rebbe?"

"Who are you?" asked Reb Zalmele.

"Don't you recognize me?" the man feigned surprise. "Remember, Rebbe, I recently shared with you a *peyres* on a Mishnah in Dmay and you mocked it with a witticism, saying my *peyres* was '*peyres dmay*.'"

For a moment, Reb Zalmele felt greatly relieved, and was about to ask the man's forgiveness. But he sensed that something wasn't right.

"Please," he said, "tell me the whole truth. Are you really the man I insulted, or are you just trying to lift my spirits? If I find out the truth later, I'll feel even worse."

These simple words so moved the fellow that he admitted that Reb Zalmele's father-in-law had sent him to enact this ploy.

Reb Zalmele kept on suffering like that until the Vilna Gaon heard about the story. The Gaon summoned him, had one of the Gaon's profound conversations with him, and lifted his spirits.

381

Reb Itsele Volozhiner was extremely careful to avoid even a hint of gossip or slander. He refused to say a negative word about anyone.

Once he found himself bound to inform others that a certain person was a liar who should not be trusted. But he didn't want the word "liar" on his tongue. So instead he declared, "That man has such a phenomenal memory! One guy can sometimes remember things that happened ten years ago. Another can remember what happened twenty years ago. People with really great memories can remember what happened fifty years ago. But this one—he remembers things that never even happened!"

384

Every morning after he prayed, Reb Moyshe Leyb Sasover would visit each widow in town and say, "Good morning!"

387

Reb Yankev Yitschok, the Chozeh of Lublin, used to say: "I detest fools. Even if I were to visit the World to Come and see a fool being driven in a grand coach, followed by thirteen wagons full of eternal life, I would run after him through all the streets, shouting: 'A fool stays a fool, I don't envy you! A fool stays a fool, I don't envy you!'"

388

Reb Naftoli Ropshitser was a real wit. He used to say: "Hell doesn't scare me. The only thing I'm afraid of is that when I get to the World to Come, they shouldn't seat me next to a fool."

391

Reb Leyzer Lipe, the father of Reb Elimelech and Reb Zushe, lived in the country. He was wealthy and extremely considerate of others. His custom when traveling to town was to offer a ride to anyone he encountered who was going on foot.

Once he met a pauper walking along with his pack on his back.

"Reb Yid," Reb Leyzer Lipe said to him, "climb on up, I'll take you to town."

"Thank you very much," answered the pauper. "I'd rather walk so that I can stop in every village, knock on doors, and make a few groshn."

"How much would you say you're likely to make in the villages? I'll give you that much, and you can ride."

But the poor man still refused. He said that he enjoyed going to the villages, visiting the houses, speaking to people.

"You know what?" Reb Leyzer Lipe asked him. "Put your pack in the wagon. I'll bring it to town and leave it in safekeeping until you arrive."

In exchange for generous alms, he managed to convince the pauper to let him bring the pack to town in his wagon.

392

Reb Yankev Berlin, Reb Hersh Leyb's father, was a prominent merchant. He used to travel to Leipzig and Königsberg and do big business. In Mir, where he lived, he kept a fine house in the manner of the wealthy of those days, and he employed a maid.

He returned from one of his trips with fine glassware for the house—the kind of thing that's never seen in our parts. His wife was delighted with the gift, and she guarded it like precious jewelry.

One day, the maid happened to break a few of the pieces. The mistress screamed at her, as rich ladies do.

"You mustn't shout at her," Reb Yankev said to his wife. "She's just as worthy as you."

"Look what she did!" his wife retorted.

"You can make a claim for damages," Reb Yankev said, "but you can't shout at her."

"That's right, I'll take her to see the rabbi," and his wife put on her shawl and told the maid to come along.

Reb Yankev got up, put on his coat and accompanied them.

"You can stay at home," his wife told him. "I can argue my case to the rabbi myself."

"I'm not going to argue for you," replied Reb Yankev. "I'm going to argue for the maid."

393

Reb Chaim Sanzer maintained a yeshiva in Sanz at his own expense. He paid the head of the yeshiva, Reb Moyshe Shmuel, 25 Austrian *reinisch* a week.

A Gentile woman once brought Reb Chaim's wife a turkey that she wanted to sell. Reb Chaim's wife bargained with her, but they couldn't settle on a price, so she didn't buy it. When the woman left the rabbi's house, Reb Moyshe Shmuel's wife caught up with her and bought the turkey.

When the rabbi's wife saw this, she was incensed, and she ran to Reb Chaim shouting, "Take a look at that charity case of yours, feasting on turkeys and stuffing Gentiles with money. The turkey was too expensive for me, but not for Moyshe Shmuel's wife."

Reb Chaim called for Reb Moyshe Shmuel's wife.

He asked her, "Why did you out-bargain my wife to get the turkey?"

"Holy Rebbe," trembled Reb Moyshe Shmuel's wife, "my husband, may he live and be well, is a weak person. He works hard in the yeshiva, and he needs some poultry to nourish himself."

"If so," said Reb Chaim, "we have to increase his pay."

And that very week, he raised Reb Moyshe Shmuel's wages.

395

Reb Nochemke of Grodno was well known for his constant involvement in charitable work.

One bitter winter night, a trustee of the Grodno community was returning from a meeting. He saw Reb Nochemke bent over from the cold, trudging through the snow. He immediately told his coachman to stop, and he invited Reb Nochemke onto the sled. Reb Nochemke was holding something against his chest.

"Rebbe," he asked, "what are you carrying there so late at night in such bitter weather?"

"A puppy," answered Reb Nochemke.

"A puppy?" wondered the man. "How'd you get a puppy, Rebbe?"

"It's like this," said Reb Nochemke. "A Gentile neighbor of mine gave birth, but the baby is weak and can't nurse. The poor mother is in agony from not being able to nurse, and she was up all night screaming. My wife said that a puppy might be able to suck out the milk. So I went to a Gentile acquaintance of mine and borrowed his puppy, and now I'm taking it to the mother."

398

Reb Zundl Salanter once traveled home from Mir, where he had been studying on his own. Jewish merchants from Memel were in the wagon with him. And since Reb Zundl dressed like a simple, poor Jew, they took him for a homeless wanderer, teased him, and played tricks on him—not unusual for people of the merchant class.

That night, they all stayed over at an inn. Reb Zundl had a bite to eat, placed his satchel at his head, and lay down on a bench for the night. The merchants ordered a nice supper, joked, and caroused like real Philistines. As their spirits rose, they decided to find the pauper who was traveling with them and have a bit of fun with him. They saw him lying on the bench sleeping, with his beard splayed out.

"Gang," one of them called, "let's really get his goat by burning off his beard."

No sooner said than done: One of them grabbed a candle and brought it near Reb Zundl's beard. The fire began to scorch his beard down to the skin.

Reb Zundl felt it and woke up. He didn't open his eyes, pretended to still be asleep, and murmured: "More... a bit more..."

A while later, the wagon arrived in Memel. The whole town came out to greet Reb Zundl with great honor. The merchants' hearts sank. They'd insulted and tormented the holy Reb Zundl!

"Rebbe," they pleaded with him, "please forgive us, we didn't know..."

"God forbid, I don't have any complaint against you," said Reb Zundl. "You got to have a little bit of fun. But I want you to solemnly swear that from this day forth, you will no longer play tricks on anyone."

402

When Reb Yisroel Salanter was widowed, he went to stay at the home of one of his close friends, Reb Yankev Moyshe Karpas, one of the rich men of Kovno.

His children noticed that Reb Yisroel performed his ritual hand-washing with only a tiny bit of water, even though there was a large container full of water in the kitchen. They were very surprised. A holy man like Reb Yisroel, wouldn't he use a full pitcher to purify himself? They told Karpas. He watched and saw that it was true: Reb Yisroel drew just enough water to cover the bottom of the pitcher, and that's all he used to wash. Karpas was amazed, too.

When they sat down at the table, Karpas gathered his nerve and asked Reb Yisroel, "Please don't take offense, Rebbe, at what I'm going to ask you. 'It is Torah, and I must learn it,' as the Talmud says. Why is it that when you purify your hands, you only use a little bit of water? I believe it says in the Shulchan Aruch that although you might get by with just a few ounces, a *reviyis* of water, one ought to enhance the mitzvah by pouring thoroughly over both hands."

"I'll tell you what happened," said Reb Yisroel, "I saw your maid carrying the water from far off, trudging uphill to your house, bent over double. And on someone's else back, you may not enhance a mitzvah."

406

Reb Mendele Slutsker was a world-class scholar, but he never wanted to become a town rabbi. For decades he studied in Isserlin's study house, directing the yeshiva and learning Torah with the "Dozen," twelve renowned scholars all supported by the wealthy Isserlin.

Every day, he and his students would go to Isserlin's house to drink tea. Reb Mendele himself would serve everyone. He brought the tea to the table, gave everyone as much as they wanted, and only when everyone else was finished would he serve himself.

Once, the fundraiser for the Mir Yeshiva came to Slutsk. The fundraiser went to see the rich man. He saw a crowd of Jews sitting around the table drinking tea, with a little Jew serving everyone. He figured, "Must be the rich man's servant." So he sat down and asked for a glass of tea. He was a portly fellow who dearly loved his tea, and he ordered glass after glass, treating Reb Mendele like a servant. The crowd watched without saying a word.

On Shabbos mornings after praying, they had the custom of coming to the rich man's house to enjoy kiddush. When the whole crowd was seated around the tables, Isserlin and Reb Mendele would come in. Everyone would stand up and wish the rich man and the head of the yeshiva, "Gut Shabbos!"

That Shabbos, the messenger from Mir went to Isserlin's house with the scholars. He saw the rich man coming in with the little Jew, and the whole crowd standing up and saying, "Gut Shabbos, Rebbe! Gut Shabbos!"

Naturally, he grew curious. "Who," he asked, "is that man?"

And the answer came, "Don't you know? That's Reb Mendele!"

His heart stopped. He had treated Reb Mendele like a servant! He rushed up to Reb Mendele, pleading, "Forgive me, Rebbe, please don't be offended, Rebbe, I didn't know."

"How did you insult me?" Reb Mendele stared at him. "For what do I need to forgive you?"

"I didn't know who you were, Rebbe," the humiliated collector said. "I ordered you around like a servant."

"I don't understand how you sinned against me or why you're asking forgiveness," Reb Mendele simply answered. "You wanted a glass of tea, and I gave it to you. On the contrary, I should be thanking you for the opportunity to do a mitzvah."

408

Reb Yosele Slonimer and his son-in-law Reb Yitschok Yankev Reines once came to Ponevezh. They went to see the rabbi, Reb Moyshe Itsl Ponevezher. Just as you'd expect, they discussed matters of Torah. All the scholars and prominent men in town came as well, to honor the visitors. Reb Yosele posed a thorny problem. Reb Moyshe Itsl tried to solve it, but couldn't. It was an incredibly difficult question, and beyond everyone's ability to answer.

When Reb Yosele and his son-in-law had returned to the privacy of their inn, Reb Yitschok Yankev turned to him and said, "Father-in-law, what did you do?"

"What do you mean?" asked Reb Yosele.

"Don't you understand?" said Reb Yitschok Yankev. "In front of the most important members of his town, you asked Reb Itsl a question he couldn't answer."

"Oh mercy, you're right! I have humiliated him..." He didn't say another word. He had fainted dead away.

409

A man came to Reb Yoshe Ber to discuss a certain topic. He was a tiresome person. He sat and droned on for far too long.

Before leaving, he said to Reb Yoshe Ber, "Rebbe, I hope you don't mind that I've taken up so much of your time."

"God forbid," responded Reb Yoshe Ber, "only a fool would mind. Indeed—I hope *you* don't mind."

410

A respected Kovno householder once lost all his money, and Reb Yitschok Elchonon went around the city with a communal leader raising funds for the poor man. The householder was well-known in town, so they agreed not to say for whom they were collecting.

Eventually, they came to the home of a rich man from whom they expected a generous contribution. The rich man enthusiastically greeted them, invited them into the living room, and asked why they had come to see him.

"We need a contribution from you," said Reb Yitschok Elchonon, "and right away. We have many more houses to visit."

"What are you collecting for?" asked the rich man.

"For an individual," answered Reb Yitschok Elchonon.

"Who?" the rich man was curious to know.

"That we can't tell you," answered Reb Yitschok Elchonon. "It's a respected member of the community who has unfortunately lost his money, and we can't leave him penniless."

The rich man thought it over. "Rebbe, I'll give you twenty-five rubles if you tell me who it is."

The community leader looked at Reb Yitschok Elchonon: twenty-five rubles is nothing to sneeze at. Reb Yitschok Elchonon didn't hesitate for a second before answering, "I can't tell you."

The rich man saw that Reb Yitschok Elchonon wasn't budging, so he said, "Rebbe, I'll give you fifty rubles."

The community leader looked again at Reb Yitschok Elchonon and said, "Rebbe, maybe... after all, fifty rubles."

Reb Yitschok Elchonon stood his ground: he wouldn't tell.

"Rebbe," the rich man said, "I'll give you 100 rubles!"

When he heard "100 rubles," the leader said to Reb Yitschok Elchonon, "Rebbe, let's tell him in secret, with a solemn oath that he won't tell anyone else. Think about it, Rebbe—100 rubles! How many doors will we have to knock on before we collect that much?"

But Reb Yitschok Elchonon wouldn't hear of it. He said to the rich man, "Please don't detain us any longer. Offer me thousands, and you still won't get the name from me. His good name is worth more than gold."

When the rich man heard that, he begged Reb Yitschok Elchonon to trouble himself to stay just a little longer and come into his private office. He asked the community leader to wait in the living room.

The rich man poured out his heart to Reb Yitschok Elchonon and told him that his own business was going badly. He was growing more desperate every day and had nowhere to look to for hope. He had often thought of going to the rabbi, but he was afraid that his secret might be found out. But now that he saw how far the rabbi would go to protect the other man's identity, he knew that he could turn to the rabbi and beg for his help.

415

Reb Yisroel Meir, the Chofetz Chaim, spent time in his youth studying in solitude in Amstiveve, a small town in the Grodno province. The town water carrier was a simple Jew, not too bright. The boys in town used to tease the water carrier, making fun of him and playing pranks.

One time during the winter, the gang of wise guys cooked up a new idea: On their way home from school every evening as they went by the town well, they would fill the bucket with water and leave it there. It would freeze solid overnight, and when the water carrier came at dawn, the first one there to draw water, he would have to chop out the ice. He used to shout, weep, and curse whoever had done this to him.

Reb Yisroel Meir found out about this. On his way home from the study house, late every night, he would first go to the well and pour the water out of the bucket.

418

A certain young Maskil used to come visit the writer Dovid Frischmann. He would linger for hours on end, jabbering on about this and that and keeping Frischmann from his work. Frischmann couldn't figure out how to get rid of his unwelcome guest.

Once while the young man was visiting him, they happened on the topic of philology. Frischmann argued that philology is nonsense, worthless, that words in and of themselves don't mean anything.

"Take, for example," said Frischmann, "the German words *auf Wiedersehen*, 'until we meet again.' But what do they actually mean? Someone says, '*auf Wiedersehen*' but is thinking, 'I hope I never see you again.'"

And with that Frischmann got up, shook the young man's hand, and said, "*Auf Wiedersehen*."

The young man never returned.

419

During his last years, when he was ill and weak, Achad Ha'am employed a private secretary. The young man would read to him, take dictation for his memoirs, and the like.

A day before he died, Achad Ha'am sensed that his last moments were approaching. He summoned the young man and said, "It's Friday. I have to pay your wages. Here's some money. Take what I owe you."

"What are you talking about?" the young man began. "That can wait..."

"No, no," Achad Ha'am insisted. "Maybe tomorrow I'll be in front of the Heavenly Court, and I don't want them to whip me for the sin of failing to pay wages on time."

420

The Dubner Maggid once paid a visit to a stingy rich man to ask for a contribution for a communal cause. The rich man refused to give. Before he left, the Dubner said to the rich man: "You should know that you have been invited to the World to Come."

"Really, Rebbe?" wondered the rich man. "Because I won't give charity, I've earned the World to Come?"

"Let me tell you a story," said the Dubner.

> In a certain town there was a stingy rich man. All his life he never gave anyone a penny. Before he died, he ordered that all of his money should be buried with him. He arrived at the Heavenly Court. They opened the book of memory—not a penny of charity was recorded there.
>
> They asked him, "Why didn't you observe the commandment to give charity?"
>
> He responded, "Down there, in the world of falsehood, where there are so many swindlers, I didn't know who I should give to. So I brought all my money to distribute here, in the True World."
>
> The court researched the relevant law and issued its ruling: "If there are two precedents like his, he merits the World to Come."
>
> They did further research, but only found one such case—Korach, who was swallowed by the earth with all his money.

"Now," concluded the Dubner, "when you come to the other world, there will be three: Korach, that other stingy rich man, and you—so you'll be invited to the World to Come."

421

The Dubner Maggid once paid a visit to a learned rich man to ask him to contribute toward the ransom money for kidnapped Jews. The rich man treated him with great respect and asked him to sit. Naturally, they began discussing matters of Torah. The Dubner related one of his own insights; the rich man, too. But since the Dubner wanted to get something done, he turned to the larger subject of charity. The rich man responded with an insight on the same topic. Then the Dubner decided to convey an insight about ransoming captives. The rich man responded in kind. The Dubner saw that he was getting nowhere, so he said to the rich man:

"I'll tell you a parable."

> Someone once made his way to a distant province. He saw that the people there didn't know about onions, and since he had a bunch of onions in his satchel, he gave it to them. When they realized how tasty food was with onions, they were so grateful for the gift that they repaid him with the weight of those onions in gold.
>
> Sometime later he visited the same distant province. By now the people there had their own onions, but they didn't know about garlic. He took a bunch of garlic out of his satchel and gave it to them, looking forward to gold in return. But the locals took his bunch of garlic and gave him back its weight in onions.

"The same thing's happening to me," said the Dubner. "I tell you one of my insights, and in return you tell me one of yours. But what I want in return is money!"

423

A woman came to see Reb Pinches, the author of the *Haflo'oh*, and complained, "Rebbe, my husband is too generous. He spends all his money on charity and free loans. It's more than he can afford."

While she was talking, a man came in and complained: "Rebbe, I'm a poor man. My family and I are starving for a piece of bread. I have a rich brother, but he pretends I don't exist."

Reb Pinches summoned the husband and the brother.

"Why do you behave like that?" he asked the first.

"Rebbe," the husband said, "I'm mortal like everybody. I don't know what will happen tomorrow—I might die! So I need to give as much charity as I can now."

Then Reb Pinches turned to the other man: "Why are you so stingy, so cruel, that you don't have pity even on your own brother?"

"Rebbe," the latter responded, "I don't know how long I'll live. I might live for a hundred years! So I have to make provisions for my old age."

"May God Almighty preserve you both," said Reb Pinches, "from the things you each fear most."

426

Reb Zalmen Uri's was one of the most well-respected Jews in Vilna. He was quite learned, very wealthy, and a generous philanthropist. His greatest commitment was to free loans. Small-scale merchants, storekeepers, tailors, and shoemakers could borrow money from him without interest so that they could do business.

Once, he was approached by a young man who wanted to borrow 100 rubles for three months. He had a chance to do a deal and make a huge profit, but he didn't have the capital. Reb Zalmen wasn't acquainted with the young man.

"Is there anyone who can serve as a guarantor for you?"

"No," answered the young man.

"Please don't be offended," said Reb Zalmen, "but I can't give you the money."

The young man stood there with tears in his eyes, getting ready to leave. Reb Zalmen was touched. He turned to the young man and asked again: "Is there really no one in the whole city who can guarantee the loan?"

"No," the young man said in anguish. "There's no one except God himself."

"Oh, if *that's* the case," rejoiced Reb Zalmen, "you've certainly got a reliable guarantor. You'll get the money."

Reb Zalmen took a piece of paper, wrote down "Loan to God who is merciful to the poor," placed it among his receipts, and counted out the hundred rubles for the young man.

Three months later, the young man came to see Reb Zalmen. He eagerly told him that thank God, the deal had gone well and he'd come to return the money.

But Reb Zalmen didn't want it. "I've already been repaid," he said.

"What?" wondered the young man.

"Your guarantor," answered Reb Zalmen, "already paid me back. God returned the loan with interest."

The young man didn't want to keep the money, so they reached a compromise: Reb Zalmen would use the money to make further free loans, and the two men would share the merit of the mitzvah.

429

Once Reb Chaim Sanzer's son Reb Boruch came to his father and complained that he was about to marry off his daughter, but he didn't have any money for the wedding.

"I don't have any money now," said Reb Chaim.

Some days later, a few of Reb Chaim's wealthy Hasidim came to see him, and before they departed, they gave him generous donations.

When the rich men had left, Reb Chaim called a certain poor Hasid of his who had two unmarried daughters. Reb Chaim gave him all the money, saying, "Here. Now you have enough to marry them off."

Some time later, Reb Boruch went to see his father.

Reb Chaim told him, "I've given away the money."

"How could you do that, Father?" Reb Boruch protested. "Do I mean less to you than a stranger? I have to marry off a daughter, too."

"You," answered Reb Chaim, "have other options. Anyone would give you money for your daughter's wedding. But nobody would give to that poor man."

431

A rich man once came to visit Reb Chaim Sanzer. Reb Chaim asked, "Do you give charity?"

"Not to boast, but I give to all the necessary causes," said the rich man.

"Go ahead and boast," said Reb Chaim, "but give a lot!"

435

Whenever Reb Nochemke of Grodno was asked to be the sandek, to hold the baby at a circumcision, he took the trouble to learn about how the father was doing. If the father didn't have the means, Reb Nochemke would pay for the refreshments and provide for the mother's needs.

A certain storekeeper once asked Reb Nochemke to be the sandek for his newborn son. Reb Nochemke had heard that even though everybody thought of the man as a stable and upstanding householder, he was actually quite down on his luck. Reb Nochemke understood that the storekeeper would be too proud to accept any money, so he went to the man and asked, "Tell me, when are you going to Warsaw?"

"What do you need in Warsaw, Rebbe?" the storekeeper asked.

"A certain acquaintance of mine is in the hospital there. I want to send him thirty rubles, but I can't send it through the mail because I don't know his exact address. So I'd like to ask you to deliver the money to him next time you're in Warsaw on business."

"But I don't know when I'll be going to Warsaw," the storekeeper hemmed and hawed.

"No rush," said Reb Nochemke. "Take the money now, and whenever you get to Warsaw you can deliver it."

The storekeeper took the thirty rubles and had enough money to take care of the mother's recovery and the circumcision.

When Reb Nochemke arrived at the circumcision, the storekeeper said to him: "Rebbe, you never gave me the name of that sick man in Warsaw."

"I forget," said Reb Nochemke. "I'll check my records."

A few months passed, and Reb Nochemke kept "forgetting" to look up the name.

Eventually things started going better for the storekeeper, and he returned the thirty rubles to Reb Nochemke with gratitude.

437

Rabbi Meir Leibush ben Yechiel Michel, known as the Malbim, once visited a certain town. During the prayers in the study house, he saw everyone kiss the Torah scroll's mantle by touching their hands to it and then bringing their fingers to their mouth. But he also saw that when a pauper came in to ask for alms, nobody gave him anything. They put him off with promises.

"You've got everything backwards," the Malbim told them. "You kiss the Torah with your hands, and you give charity with your mouths. You should kiss the Torah with your mouths and give charity with your hands."

439

Reb Sholem Kaminker once approached a stingy rich man to ask for a contribution in support of a poor man from a respectable family. Naturally, the miser didn't want to give anything.

"I have enough poor relatives already," he grumbled.

"And why not finish your sentence?" said Reb Sholem.

"What do you mean, Rebbe?"

"Oh, just that you should complete the rest of your thought out loud: '…and if I don't give anything to my own relatives, what makes you think I'll give to a stranger?'"

442

In Vilna there was a Jew—Shimen Kaftan was his name. He was a simple, honest Jew who devoted himself to helping others. He would walk around the city all day raising money to support all the full-time scholars and poor young students. All Vilna knew Shimen Kaftan, and wherever he went, he would never leave empty-handed.

One time, he went to see a rich man to ask for a contribution. A young man, a bit of a prankster, happened to be there as well, and he decided to have a little fun with this simple, honest Jew.

"Reb Shimen," he declared, "I'll give you 100 rubles, on condition that you sell me your share of the World to Come."

Shimen stood there and thought it over. He answered, "Yes, I'll sell it to you."

"Good," replied the other fellow, driving a hard bargain. "But I want you to sign on the dotted line."

"Yes," said Shimen, "signed and sealed, it'll be yours."

Everybody watched with great interest as pen and paper were brought. A document of sale was drafted in great detail. Shimen signed it, witnesses added their signatures, and Shimen received his 100 rubles in cash.

The sale was the talk of Vilna. A Jew selling his place in the World to Come!—the world had never heard of such a thing. Everyone kept asking Shimen, "How could you do such a thing, Shimen? Selling your portion of the World to Come?"

"What's the problem?" Shimen innocently replied. "Do I need a place in the World to Come in order to raise money for my scholars?"

443

When Reb Yoshe Ber was the rabbi of Slutsk, a Jewish coachman once came to him before Passover, weeping bitterly. "My rotten fate, Rebbe. All winter I was without work, haven't earned a penny. And now, before Passover, when there are things to be delivered and I can earn money for the holiday, my horse collapsed and died."

"Go into my stall," said Reb Yoshe Ber. "Take my cow to the marketplace and exchange it for a horse."

The coachman was overjoyed. He went straight to the stall, removed the rabbi's cow, and walked away with her.

A while later, the rabbi's wife went into the stall to see to the cow—gone! She ran into the house shouting, "Yoshe Ber, our cow's been stolen!"

"It wasn't stolen," Reb Yoshe Ber responded quietly, "she's still here."

"Where is she?"

"If the man didn't exchange her yet, he still has her," he sternly answered.

She stared at him. "What man? What exchange?"

Reb Yoshe Ber explained to her that he had given the cow to a poor Jew so that he could earn his living. She grew angry and started shouting, "How could you do that? She was our only cow. Now where will we find a drop of milk?"

"Look at it this way," answered Reb Yoshe Ber. "You have bread, and on top of that you want milk, while this poor Jew doesn't even have bread? Now, you tell me: is that fair?"

447

There was a young simpleton in Ponedel who used to go around barefoot, like a madman. Reb Chaim, the town rabbi, bought him a pair of shoes.

A few days later, he saw the boy was still walking barefoot.

"Where are your shoes?" he asked.

"I don't know how to put them on," the boy answered simply.

Reb Chaim took him home and put the shoes on his feet.

From that day on, every morning Reb Chaim would go to put the boy's shoes on and every night to take them off.

450

Reb Tsvi Hersh Vodislaver, Reb Simcha Bunim's father, was famous for his hospitality. His home was open to all. When a guest came, he would give him food, drink, and a place to sleep, all with great respect and an open heart.

One winter night, a group of guests came. As usual, Reb Hersh cheerfully greeted them, ordered the table set, and brought out his best food and drink for the guests. The guests started eating, drinking, and having a wonderful time.

Reb Hersh saw that they were exhausted and would soon need a place to lie down. He called over his son and said, "My dear Simcha Bunim, I want you to come up with something new concerning the matter of hospitality."

Simcha Bunim left the room, and it was some while before he returned. "So, did you make something up?" his father asked.

"Yes."

The guests assumed that he was about to share a new Torah insight with them. Reb Hersh said to the guests, "Let's see what my son came up with."

And he took them to a large room, where beds had been made up for them.

454

Some poor strangers arrived one Friday afternoon in Lenshits, where Reb Chaim Auerbach was the rabbi. Everyone refused to take in these unexpected guests for Shabbos.

The paupers came to Reb Chaim and complained, "Rebbe, no

one has invited us for Shabbos."

Reb Chaim stood up, put on his Shabbos coat and his fur hat, and said to the guests, "Come, let's go to Ozerkov, a nearby town, and we'll spend Shabbos there."

When the crowd in the marketplace saw the rabbi walking with the paupers, everyone started shouting, "Rebbe, where are you going?"

"I'm going to Ozerkov," Reb Chaim answered. "In a town where no one is willing to take in a guest, I don't want to be rabbi."

Everyone was ashamed and immediately ran to be the first to invite a guest.

456

Reb Rifoel of Bershad was profoundly humble. He didn't have even a sixtieth of the pride of the usual Torah scholar. He used to say: "Praise and thanks to the Almighty for making arrogance a sin. If, God forbid, arrogance were a commandment, how could I carry out the will of the Creator? How can I summon up even a scrap of arrogance, when I am but dust and ashes?"

459

A man once came to see Reb Zalmen Poyzner, the rabbi of Warsaw and author of the *Khemdas Shlomo*. The visitor complained about his family's strained circumstances and explained that he had a rich relative in Kutno whom he wanted the rabbi to persuade to help him out.

Reb Zalmen wrote him the letter, and the man set off with it for Kutno. His rich relative was deeply impressed to receive a letter from the rabbi of Warsaw, and he greeted his distant cousin like a close friend. But when he actually read the letter, he couldn't believe his eyes. Reb Zalmen had given his poor relative, a simple Jew, grand titles and honorifics as though he were the greatest sage of his generation. So he took the letter to his rabbi, the rabbi of Kutno,

Reb Moyshe Aren. The rabbi was also puzzled.

"You know what," Reb Moyshe Aren said to the rich man, "the next time you go to Warsaw, go see Reb Zalmen and discuss it with him."

The rich man traveled to Warsaw and went to see Reb Zalmen. He explained that he was the Kutno relative to whom the rabbi had written, and he had helped out his cousin just as the rabbi had asked. He said to the rabbi: "Please don't be offended at what I'm going to ask you, Rabbi. How could you give him such a letter?"

"Meaning what?" asked Reb Zalmen.

"You have to ask?" said the rich man. "You called him 'rabbi,' 'genius,' 'saint,' and the like."

"Oh, wouldn't you know it, but they say the same things about me," Reb Zalmen replied with great simplicity. He got up, went to the sideboard, took out a number of letters, and brought them over to his guest: "Here, see?"

The rich man was impressed: Such humility!

When he got back home to Kutno, he went to see Reb Moyshe Aren and told him the story. Reb Moyshe Aren didn't want to believe it. It was just incredible that a man should be so free of self-regard.

"I'm going to go to Warsaw and see for myself whether Reb Zalmen is really so humble."

Reb Moyshe Aren went to see Reb Zalmen. Reb Zalmen greeted him warmly and ordered refreshments. Reb Moyshe Aren refused to touch a thing and put on a stern face. "What good are these trifles? I'd rather you honored me by presenting some of your renowned teachings."

Reb Zalmen obediently explained a subtle point in Torah scholarship.

When he finished, Reb Moyshe Aren said to him: "I guess you behave like a salesman. First you show me the cheap stuff. Now, give me a really good piece of Torah."

Reb Zalmen related an even more brilliant insight.

The rabbi of Kutno listened and said, "You call that good? It's even worse than the first. Come on, give me a real piece of Torah."

"Believe me," Reb Zalmen said with great humility, "that's the best I can do."

The rabbi of Kutno was deeply moved. He begged Reb Zalmen's forgiveness and confessed that he had only been testing him.

461

When Reb Yisroel Salanter fell ill in Königsberg, the leaders of the community used to come visit him. They took care of all his needs and wouldn't leave his bedside.

As he grew dangerously feeble, they noticed that the clock on the wall ticked too loudly and was disturbing him. So they agreed to take the clock out into another room.

Reb Yisroel overheard that, and he shook his head: "Ay, Jews, a poor old man is sick, and you want to turn the whole world upside down on his account? Just listen, the horses are also loudly clopping on the cobblestones—next thing, you'll be ordering that they cover the streets with straw."

462

Once, a simple Jew, an ignoramus, came to see Reb Yoshe Ber with his small child and said: "Rebbe, my boy is learning Chumash already. I want you to quiz him."

Everyone present was mystified at the nerve of that ignoramus. He couldn't find anyone else to test his little student other than the leading scholar of the generation? But Reb Yoshe Ber was good-natured, so he asked the boy a few questions and then said to the father: "I only wish that what one can say of your child, one will be able to say of my children as well."

The Jew went away glowing with pride.

"Rebbe, what did you see in the child that made you wish it could be said of your own children?"

"Simple," answered Reb Yoshe Ber. "I wish that people will say of my children that they know more than their father."

466

One Friday afternoon, Reb Chaim Brisker was in the bath house. Several others were sitting around and chatting.

"What a stingy guy the owner here is," one of them complained. "Look at all these leaky water buckets."

"But of course they're leaky!" replied Reb Chaim with a smile. "A leaky bucket has several advantages: you can pour more water in it; it's not as heavy; and you don't even need to flip it over to pour the water out!"

467

Reb Zalmele, Reb Chaim Volozhiner's brother, was a brilliant scholar and a gentle soul.

One Friday afternoon, coming out of the baths, he discovered that his shirt had been stolen. He didn't say a word and went back home.

"Zalmele," his wife asked him, "where's your shirt?"

"Someone mistook mine for theirs," he explained.

"So," she asked him, "where's *his* shirt?"

"Oh, his shirt?" Reb Zalmele guilelessly replied. "He must have forgotten to leave it behind."

463

Reb Shmuel Salant, the rabbi of Jerusalem, was known to be quick-witted. He once had a dispute with a bully, a real piece of work. His antagonist lost all sense of propriety and shouted at Reb Shmuel, "Rebbe, I'll smash your windows!"

"And you think I'll just sit here and take it, do you?" Reb Shmuel replied with a dark look.

The bully puffed up even further. "What exactly are you going to do about it, huh?"

"What do you mean?" smiled Reb Shmuel. "Right away I'll get a glazier to fix the windows."

464

Reb Chaim Yankev of Virdevits, the rabbi of Moscow, was born with a stutter.

He once had a dispute with a stubborn opponent. The latter lost his temper and began cursing Reb Chaim Yankev with every curse known to Jews. "You're a liar, a sneak, a brazen dog!"—and the like.

"A-a-and y-y-you," Reb Chaim Yankev stammered, "a-a-are a st-st-stutterer."

"*I'm* a stutterer?!?" the other laughed derisively.

"Listen to me," said Reb Chaim Yankev. "If you're going to tell me what *you* are, I'll tell you what *I* am."

465

While Reb Chaim Brisker was attending the big rabbinical assembly in St. Petersburg, the reporters for the Jewish newspapers wrote a great deal about him. As usual, they reported all sorts of wild exaggerations which had utterly no basis. The reporter for the Warsaw *Haynt* devoted more time than anyone else to writing about Reb Chaim, while totally fabricating quotes from him. Of course Reb Chaim detested this.

Once, the reporter for the *Haynt* came to interview Reb Chaim.

"I haven't yet read today's *Haynt*," smiled Reb Chaim, "so I don't know yet what I am going to say."

469

Reb Meir Michl Shater was by nature taciturn. He barely spoke when at home with his family. In general, he did not get involved in domestic matters, preferring to devote all his time to Torah and prayer.

One evening, close to the holiday of Sukkes, his son was ordered to report for military conscription. His wife pleaded with him: "Meir Michl, what's going to happen? We have to do something.

Somehow we have to save our son from Gentile hands."

Reb Meir Michl was silent. His wife went on, speaking passionately, like a mother—but Reb Meir Michl said not a word.

Suddenly he stood up, walked over to the window, and stood there, looking outside. His wife waited, thinking: He must be trying to think up a way to save our son. A while passed like this, he standing and looking, she silent and waiting.

"Nu, Meir Michl," she finally asked him, "what have you come up with?"

Reb Meir Michl looked out the window and spoke as if to himself:

"Tonight would have been our very last opportunity this month to bless the new moon, but it isn't even visible."

470

Reb Rifoel Volozhiner, Reb Hersh Leyb's son in law, spent all his waking hours studying Torah. He didn't even get involved in family matters. His wife was the mistress of the house. She oversaw its daily needs, arranged marriages for their children, granted dowries, and provided meals to yeshiva students.

Reb Rifoel paid absolutely no attention to these things. If a child of his was being given away in marriage, they would let him know an hour before the wedding. He'd close his Talmud, don his Shabbos finery, and go to the chuppah.

One time, he was called to go to the chuppah for a child of his. As he was putting on his silk kaftan, his sleeve snagged on his elbow.

"Ah," he sighed, "it's so hard, raising children!"

471

Reb Rifoel knew little about the outside world.

One time, people were trying to persuade him to go take a walk. They explained that walking was healthy.

"Sure, it's healthy," conceded Reb Rifoel, "but where does it get you? You still have to come back."

472

One time, Reb Rifoel was sitting and eating. A plate full of stewed cherries lay on the table. Reb Rifoel contemplated the dish for a while, then ate it all up and pronounced with great satisfaction, "Such delicious beans!"

473

Ref Rifoel was a quiet man by nature. He almost never opened up his mouth in company. People would say about him:

"Reb Rifoel keeps silent until it tires him out, then he rests up a little, and then—he stays silent some more."

474

Everyone in Jerusalem knew Reb Hirsh Michl as a gentle and righteous soul. Reb Yehoshua Leyb Diskin, the Chief Rabbi of Jerusalem, relied on Reb Hirsh Michl's prayers to intercede in Heaven for the ill and distraught.

His whole life, Reb Hirsh Michl occupied himself with Torah study and prayer. Every night, he would go to the Western Wall to recite the optional midnight service. He lived in the Old City and for thirty years never once set foot beyond its walls, not even to attend a wedding or circumcision.

When Kaiser Wilhelm was about to arrive in Jerusalem and everyone got ready to go out to see the Kaiser, Reb Hirsh Michl worried that he might be obligated to leave the Old City to take advantage of the opportunity to utter the rare blessing, "...who grants from His glory," said only when one sees a ruler in person. He thought it over, searched in the holy books for an answer to his question—but was totally stumped.

It happened that just then, on his way to the Western Wall, he fell and broke his foot.

"Praise God!" he called out with joy, "that answers the question."

475

Reb Yitschok Yankev Reines, the rabbi of Lida, was well-known as a major Zionist activist. He would travel to Zionist gatherings and congresses, where he occupied an honored position.

At one such Zionist congress, with Reb Yitschok Yankev sitting at the head of the dais, there was a heated debate about the Jewish National Fund. The assembled delegates argued at length. Finally, when the discussion had ended and it was time to vote, Reb Yitschok Yankev stood up and requested the floor.

"I regret very much, Herr Rabbi," the chairman David Wolfson said in German, "that the debate is closed. You may only speak regarding the agenda."

"Yes," answered Reb Yitschok Yankev in Yiddish, "I wish to speak about the agenda."

And he launched into a full-on rabbinic sermon.

A good while had passed, and Reb Yitzchok Yankev was just starting to get to his point.

"Excuse me, Herr Rabbi, this"—the chairman could no longer restrain himself—"is *nicht* regarding the agenda."

"Is *not* regarding the agenda," Reb Yitzchok Yankev said in Yiddish with a dismissive wave of the hand, and launched right back into his sermon.

476

The great philosopher and poet Reb Avraham ibn Ezra was an absolute pauper. Not a single venture of his worked out. Every deal went south.

Ibn Ezra himself used to say:

"Were I to sell candles, then the sun would never set; were I to sell funeral shrouds—no one would ever die."

477

The Jewish philosopher Moses Mendelssohn worked, as everybody knows, his whole life as a bookkeeper for a wealthy merchant in Berlin. As it happens, the merchant was a coarse fellow, a real ignoramus, but nonetheless did great business and employed many clerks and servants.

"See," one of Mendelssohn's confidantes once pointed out, "how unjust the world is. You're so learned, but you work for him, while that lout does big business and is incredibly rich."

"On the contrary!" Mendelssohn replied. "See how justly God rules the world. I've studied, so I can be a bookkeeper and make a living. But if my boss, that poor soul, weren't already rich, what would he do?"

478

The personal assistant of the Chasam Sofer, the head of the yeshiva of Pressburg, had an uncle who was a banker. The assistant thought very highly of himself: look at me, the personal assistant to the Chasam Sofer, and with a rich uncle to boot!

"What makes you think you're such a big shot?" the Chasam Sofer once scolded him. "It would be one thing if you knew as much as me and you had as much money as your uncle—then you'd have something to boast about. But you only know as much as your uncle and you only have as much money as me."

479

A wealthy disciple once visited Reb Dovidl Tolner. The Rebbe sat with him for a couple of hours in his private chamber. When the rich disciple left, a poor one came in. The Rebbe said a few words and then dismissed him. The pauper resented it.

"Eh, Rebbe," he said, "favoritism, God forbid, is that it?"

"Don't be silly," answered Reb Dovidl. "When you walk in, I know you're a pauper. But him? It took me a few hours until I could be absolutely sure that he's just as much a pauper as you."

480

Reb Boruch Mordche Shedlitser used to say:

"What an upside-down world it is: The rich man has money, but everybody lends to him. The poor man has nothing, but nobody will lend to him. The truth is, it should be the opposite: The wealthy man, who has cash in hand, nobody needs to lend to; the pauper, who has no cash, everyone should lend to. And what if you lend to a pauper and don't get paid back? Nu, what's the big problem? *You'll* become the pauper, and then everyone will lend to *you!*"

481

There once was a wealthy businessman in Vilna, a government supplier, Reb Shloyme Pomerants. Several families lived off his charity.

But the wheel turned, and Reb Shloyme became a complete pauper. He lost his entire fortune on a government contract gone sour. As usually happens in these situations, his friends distanced themselves from him and didn't want anything to do with him.

But soon enough the wheel turned again, and Reb Shloyme returned to his prior wealth and high standing. His friends started slinking their way back in.

Holiday-time, Shavuos it was, they all came to bid him a happy holiday. When Reb Shloyme saw them through the window, he ordered his money chest set on the dining room table. His friends came in, saw the chest on the table, and cried out in surprise, "Reb Shloyme, what's going on?"

"This is my money," he said with a smile. "You obviously came to bid a happy holiday to my money, not to me."

482

Reb Eliyahu Chaim was a tireless advocate for the communal needs of Lodz. Whenever a need arose in the city, he would visit the philanthropists and raise the necessary funds.

One year the winter was especially bitter in Lodz. It was terribly cold, and the snow lay deep. Wood was expensive and work hard to find. The paupers froze half to death. So Reb Eliyahu Chaim went out into the city to find wood for the poor.

As usual, his first visit was to the wealthiest man in his community, Poznanski. He walked into the foyer, and the butler announced him to Poznanski, who ran out to greet him:

"Oh, Rebbe! How are you, sir? Come in."

And he invited the rabbi to come into his beautiful salon, where it was light and warm.

Reb Eliyahu Chaim was in no rush. He stood there in the cold foyer and launched into a discussion about various secular communal matters. Poznanski stood there talking in his house robes, his teeth chattering. But he didn't complain: respect for the rabbi! Reb Eliyahu Chaim kept talking, discussing one topic and then the next—all very pleasantly, as if he were sitting in the light and warmth. Poznanski was soon overcome by the cold. He begged Reb Eliyahu Chaim, "Rebbe, have pity on me, come inside to the salon, I'm freezing."

"Now," replied Reb Eliyahu Chaim, "I will tell you what I came here to ask for. What a bitter winter it is, the cold is terrible, work is hard to find, and our paupers are freezing. I want you to donate wood."

Poznanski agreed immediately to make a generous donation. Only then did Reb Eliyahu Chaim walk into the salon with him.

In the course of their conversation, Poznanski asked him:

"Tell me, Rebbe, why did you stand in the foyer for so long? You could have come into the living room as usual and told me what you needed."

"Here's how it is," answered Reb Eliyahu Chaim. "The saying goes:

'The full belly does not believe the empty one.' I came here to ask for wood for the poor, who, alas, are freezing from the cold. How could you, sitting here in the salon in such sweet warmth, know what cold means? Only once you had stood for a while in the cold foyer and felt a drop of what cold is could I tell you why I came."

484

Reb Yisroel Meir, the Chofetz Chaim, was penniless in his younger years before he had written his first book. During the week, he used to sit upstairs in the section that on Shabbos belonged to the women. There he studied Torah night and day, literally making do with bread and water. Everyone in town knew of his poverty and wanted to help out any way they could, but he wouldn't hear of it. He didn't want to rely on anyone's charity.

His mother once complained to him, "Yisroel Meir, look at how we're living. Not even a piece of bread. People want to help out. Why do you have to be this way?"

"Let me tell you, Mama," he answered. "People are eager to give to me, as long as they know I won't accept; as soon as I accept, they'll stop giving."

486

Reb Moyshe Aren, the rabbi of Kutno, dedicated himself to charity. He constantly went around the city, collecting for the needy. Naturally, he didn't have it easy collecting from the rich. The poor responded more generously and willingly than the wealthy. So he had a saying:

"When I visit a poor man, I spit on the floor. But when I go to a wealthy man, the floor is covered in carpets, so the only thing to do is spit in his face."

488

When Reb Moyshe Isserles's first wife died, he delivered a grand eulogy, displaying remarkable acuity and breadth of scholarship, and impressed the audience.

His father-in-law, Reb Shachne, had another daughter, and Reb Moyshe proposed to marry her. Reb Shachne refused.

"I'm through with you as a son-in-law," he said. "If you were composed enough to deliver such an incredible eulogy for your own wife, you couldn't have really loved her."

493

Reb Yoshe Ber made a match between one of his sons and the daughter of a wealthy man. Naturally, the rich man provided a generous dowry and lavish gifts. No big deal: just a son of Reb Yoshe Ber! The young groom noticed this and became a bit conceited.

"You silly child," Reb Yoshe Ber rebuked him. "Why are you so impressed with yourself? Do you really think we're getting the dowry on your account? You're mistaken. The dowry is on my account. And why wasn't it more? That's *your* doing!"

497

As a child, the famous sage Reb Yoynesn Prager had already begun to display his great intellectual gifts, and leading scholars enjoyed speaking with him.

When Reb Yoynesn was just five years old, a very prominent rabbi came to visit his father. The guest was charmed by the little Yoynesn and would often chat with him.

Once he asked the boy: "Tell me, Yoynesn, what did you eat today?"

"Bread and—", in the middle of answering, the rabbi was called away.

Many years passed before the rabbi next encountered Reb

Yoynesn. He greeted him and immediately asked, "And what?"

"And butter," replied Reb Yoynesn without blinking.

501

When the Rebbe Reb Avrom Yehoshua Heshl of Apt was just a young boy, he once went into the kitchen and espied a roast chicken. Without hesitation he grabbed a leg and ate it up. Delicious.

At the dinner table, the chicken was served with only one leg. Everybody knew who was responsible.

"Heshele, where's the other leg?" asked his father.

"The chicken only had one leg," answered Heshl.

A few days later, Heshl and his father were on their way to the study house. He saw a chicken standing on one leg, with the other leg tucked under its feathers.

"Look, Papa," said Heshl. "There's another one-legged chicken."

"Scat!" shouted his father, and shooed off the chicken, which stuck out its other leg and ran away.

"You see," he said to Heshl, "this chicken *also* has two feet."

"And if only you had shooed the other chicken," retorted Heshl, "it would have stuck out its other leg, too."

504

By the time Reb Akiva Eiger was 15 years old, he was already famous as a prodigy in Torah. His father, Reb Moyshe Ginz, sent him to study at the Breslau yeshiva, where Reb Moyshe's father-in-law, Reb Zavl, was the rosh yeshiva. Once he was there, they began suggesting matches for him.

Of all the possible matches, Reb Akiva liked best the one with the daughter of Reb Yitschok Margolis of Lissa, a wealthy, learned man whose only daughter was modest and highly accomplished. The prospective in-laws agreed to meet at a town near Breslau.

Reb Yitschok brought along two scholars in order to test the bridegroom on his learning, as was the custom. The scholars began discussing various aspects of Torah with the bridegroom, asking questions, resolving them, showing how sharp they were—but Reb Akiva just sat there without saying a single word, like a complete ignoramus. Everyone was taken aback, and it looked like the match would be called off.

Reb Akiva's father ushered him into a side room and asked, "What happened to you, Akiva? Didn't you understand what they were discussing?"

"To you, Father, I can tell the truth," answered Reb Akiva. "One of them asked a question that Tosafos had already brought up and resolved centuries ago. The other one didn't even understand the plain meaning of the text. I didn't want to point out their errors and embarrass them. Better the match should be called off than I should embarrass an elderly Jew."

508

Reb Chaim Brisker and Reb Zalmen Sender Shapiro were friends. Both studied under Reb Yoshe Ber in their youth.

Once Reb Yoshe Ber asked his son, "Tell me, Chaimke, which one of you is a better scholar—you or Zalmen Sender?"

"Father," said Reb Chaim, "I can't answer that. Were I to say it's me, I'd be arrogant. But if I say it's Zalmen Sender, then I'd be a liar."

Reb Zalmen Sender heard this and said to Reb Chaim, "And I say you're arrogant *and* a liar!"

898

Reb Yitschokl Hamburger opposed Reb Yisroel Ba'al Shem. He fiercely battled against the Ba'al Shem Tov's Hasidic movement and constantly criticized him. The Baal Shem Tov, for his part, deeply respected Reb Yitschokl's saintliness and learning.

When the Ba'al Shem learned that Reb Yitschokl liked to criticize him, he began sending his followers to Reb Yitschokl to criticize the Ba'al Shem in order to delight Reb Yitschokl.

900

Reb Moyshe Leyb Sasover was good-hearted. He couldn't stand to see a Jew suffer. He was ready to sacrifice body and soul for another Jew's sake.

Once, when he was a young man staying with Reb Shmelke of Nikolsburg, he was sitting and learning in the study house. He heard one poor Jew confide to another: "I have no idea what to do. I have a daughter, already an old maid, and I can't marry her off. I know that no man is going to want to live with her, because she's ugly and not too bright. Anybody would be fine at this point, as long as they can put a roof over her head. But I obviously don't have a penny to my name. I know my daughter is going to remain single until she has gray hair."

Reb Moyshe Leyb called the town marriage broker and told him to go arrange a marriage for him with the poor man's daughter.

The marriage broker stared at him. Reb Moyshe Leyb, the promising young scholar, who could marry into a wealthy family, get a dowry of thousands and lifetime support to sit and learn—this Moyshe Leyb wanted to marry a poor old maid? He had to be joking.

But no, Reb Moyshe Leyb insisted that he meant it. He wanted to be that Jew's son-in-law.

The marriage broker went to the poor Jew and arranged the match with Reb Moyshe Leyb.

The poor man couldn't believe his ears. How could he wind up with a son-in-law like Reb Moyshe Leyb? And how could his daughter, an old maid, no dowry, and ugly and dull too, become Reb Moyshe Leyb's wife?

The marriage broker told him that Reb Moyshe Leyb was willing to marry his daughter just as she was, without dowry or a promise of future support.

In short, the marriage was arranged. Reb Moyshe Leyb married the poor man's daughter.

When Reb Moyshe Leyb's parents heard about it, they immediately came to town, trying to convince Reb Moyshe Leyb he'd made a terrible mistake. But Reb Moyshe Leyb just couldn't stand to see the poor Jew suffering.

It took a lot for his parents to convince him to divorce the woman.

907

Reb Mordche Meltser, the rabbi of Lida, didn't like to eat in front of anyone except his close family and friends.

The head of the community was once sitting with him and discussing communal matters. When it came time to eat, the table was set. Reb Mordche sat still and didn't get up to wash his hands for the meal.

"Rebbe," said the head of the community, "why don't you wash?"

"I'll tell you," said Reb Mordche. "Friday evening, when a Jew comes home from synagogue with the two accompanying angels, he greets them joyfully before starting his meal. He says with great feeling: 'Welcome, accompanying angels! Come in peace! Bless me with peace!' And then right away, he excuses them, and says, 'Go in peace.' Why? Because when you're sitting down to eat, a stranger—even an angel—doesn't belong."

916

Reb Chaim Brisker's home was open to all.

A visitor once came in and stole Reb Chaim's silver tobacco canister. Reb Chaim's family saw the man putting the canister in his pocket. They wanted to pat him down, but Reb Chaim wouldn't let them.

When the man left, Reb Chaim said, "Listen, if there had been any doubt about whether he had taken it, it might have been worthwhile to check. But since we know for sure he took it, why humiliate a fellow Jew?"

918

The Jewish philosopher Moses Mendelssohn loved sweets.

Someone once challenged him, "How can you? Everybody knows the saying, 'fools love sweets.'"

Mendelssohn smiled. "The clever ones thought that up so the fools would leave the sweets for us."

921

Reb Leyb, the Shpoler Zeyde, always gave generously to whoever needed it. He would even give to thieves.

The people in his town of Zlotopole didn't get it.

"How can you give away money to thieves?"

"Don't you worry," answered Reb Leyb. "Sometimes the heavenly gates of mercy are sealed. Then I send my thieves, and they pick the lock for us."

927

Reb Ayzl Kharif was once asked, "Why is a rich man always more willing to give money to a poor cripple than to a poor scholar?"

"Very simple," answered Reb Ayzl. "There's no telling whether the rich man might, God forbid, become a cripple; but for sure he's never going to become a scholar."

933

When Reb Shneur Zalman, the first Lubavitcher Rebbe, became famous, throngs of people started coming to him to receive his guidance.

Once, Reb Shneur Zalman was sitting and looking out the window. He saw a crowd of Jews coming to see him. He became terrified and started shouting: "What do they want from me? Why do they come? What do they see in me?"

"Calm down," said the rebbetzin sensibly. "It's not because of you. They just want you to tell them stories of your teacher, the holy Maggid of Mezritsh."

"Oh, really?" replied Reb Shneur Zalman. "They come so I can tell them stories? Stories? Well, I can do that."

939

Reb Shimshen, Reb Meshulem Pressburger's father, lived in Buczacz. He was an honest Jew, simple and fair. Next door lived an innkeeper who wasn't so careful about keeping Shabbos. He had decided for himself that it was all right to make money on Shabbos as long as the customer threw the coins directly into the cash box, so that he wouldn't need to actually touch it. Reb Shimshen reprimanded him, and reprimanded him again. But the innkeeper didn't change his ways. Reb Shimshen went to the rabbi and summoned the innkeeper to a hearing.

When the innkeeper heard that Reb Shimshen had summoned him to a hearing, he was shocked—what standing could Reb Shimshen possibly have in the case? They'd never done any business with each other!

When they met with the rabbi, Reb Shimshen argued: "Since we are well aware that in a place where Shabbos is desecrated fires tend to break out, I demand one of two things from my neighbor: either he agrees to stop desecrating, or he buys me out of my house, which is next to his."

940

When Reb Akiva Eiger married off his son, Reb Volf, there were many notables present—rabbis, scholars, Jewish leaders. The son was a talented scholar in his own right, and at the groom's table he gave a lecture that displayed deep insight and broad knowledge, befitting a son of Reb Akiva Eiger and befitting that distinguished crowd.

After the lecture, Reb Akiva Eiger asked the father of the bride: "Well, my dear in-law, how do you like the groom?"

"The groom is fine, I guess," the other man teased, "but I don't care for his father at all."

"You don't?" Reb Akiva Eiger replied with real anguish. "Please tell me what flaw you've noticed, and I'll repent and improve it."

The father of the bride saw that Reb Akiva Eiger had taken his joke seriously. He deeply regretted it and tried to explain, "No, Rebbe, I was just trying to have a little laugh."

"Huh? Playing the buffoon, are you? Then I shouldn't be sitting next to you." And he got up and left the table.

944

Reb Rifoel Volozhiner was famously constrained in his speech. He used to say about himself: "People think I can't talk. No—I know how to be silent."

945

A boorish nouveau-riche once wanted to acquire the status of a better family by marrying off his child to them, so he sent a marriage broker to see Reb Yankele Orenstein, the rabbi of Lemberg. "Let the rich man come himself," Reb Yankele said.

The rich man came. They made some small talk until they came to the business at hand.

"If you'll give 100,000 rubles," said Reb Yankele, "we'll be in-laws."

"Rebbe," said the rich man, taken aback, "it's true that you're very learned and have distinguished ancestors, and that's why I want my child to marry yours. But how can such a modest person as you think that your Torah and your ancestry are worth such a king's ransom?"

"God forbid!" retorted Reb Yankele. "I know very well that my Torah and ancestry are but vanity of vanities. So I'm willing to make you a trade: my vanity of vanities for your vanity of vanities."

956

Before Reb Tevele, Reb Hirsh Berliner's son, became a rabbi, he was a merchant. He would travel to the Leipzig fair and buy thousands of thalers worth of goods and wares. As merchants do, he would borrow money to make the purchases. When he came back, he would pay back what he had borrowed and borrow again. This went on for a number of years.

A man named Manele used to travel to Leipzig with him. This Manele was a wealthy, successful merchant, God-fearing and charitable, but he was unlearned and came from a simple family. His only child was a daughter. He wanted to marry her to Reb Tevele's son Reb Leybele. But he knew that the match wasn't for him. How could he, such an ignoramus, be related to Reb Tevele, who was a great scholar in his own right, in addition to being the son of the rabbi of Berlin? Manele came up with an idea.

Once when he and Reb Tevele arrived in Leipzig, he went to see the local merchants with whom Reb Tevele did business, and, pretending to confide in them, said: "You should know that Reb Tevele's got cash flow problems. I mention it to you purely out of friendly concern."

Reb Tevele met with a merchant, paid what he owed, and handed him a list of what he wanted to buy as always. But the merchant said he could no longer extend him credit. The same happened with all the other merchants Reb Tevele regularly dealt with.

Reb Tevele was entirely despondent. It seemed he would have to go home empty-handed, unable to earn a living.

Manele asked him, "What's with you, Reb Tevele? Why so gloomy?"

Reb Tevele explained the situation.

"Wickedness!" Reb Manele, exclaimed, feigning shock. "How could they behave like that? Doing good business with you for years and then all of a sudden this insult. But," he sighed, "it seems there's nothing you can do. You'll just have to pay them cash."

"What are you talking about?" retorted Reb Tevele. "Where will

I get money here in Leipzig?"

"Don't worry," smiled Manele, "I'll give you as much cash as you need."

Reb Tevele breathed easier.

"But on one condition," added Manele.

"What's that?"

"You marry your son to my daughter."

Reb Tevele was speechless. Manele—his in-law? "Let me think it over," he entreated.

Several days passed. Reb Tevele walked around the city, thinking and thinking, and couldn't decide what to do. It was almost time to go home, but he had neither goods nor money. He went to Manele and said he agreed to the deal. They formally agreed, and Reb Tevele got his money. He bought goods for cash, and the two prospective in-laws went home.

On the way, they stopped in Berlin and went to see Reb Hirsh. Reb Hirsh was happy to see his son, and when he heard about the match, he wished both of them "Mazel tov!" He invited them to stay for Shabbos.

At the Friday night table, Reb Hirsh spoke words of Torah. Reb Tevele commented in turn, and they went back and forth, as scholars do. Manele sat silently. Reb Hirsh understood that the prospective in-law was—poor man—an ignoramus.

He called his son into his private room and scolded him. "What's going on, Tevele? Why aren't you going to marry Leybele to the daughter of a scholar?"

Reb Tevele told him what had happened in Leipzig. He didn't have a choice. Reb Hirsh kept silent.

On Saturday evening after havdalah, Reb Hirsh called in his son and Manele. He handed Manele all the money he had given Reb Tevele, except for half of the dowry which he kept as a fine. The match was dissolved.

When Manele heard this, he fainted dead away.

"Well," said Reb Hirsh, "if the Torah is so precious to him that he's willing to perish for the sake of marrying his daughter to a learned family, I guess he's worthy to be related to me by marriage."

And with that, the match went through.

A while later, Reb Hirsh remarked to Reb Tevele with a smile: "You needed the money, I understand it. But the angel in heaven who arranges all marriages—I can't understand him. He didn't need the money—how could he go and make such a match?"

957

Reb Velvele, the Maggid of Vilna, took Reb Elye Dretshiner, the *Ayin Eliyahu*, as a son-in-law. Reb Velvele promised to contribute three hundred rubles as a dowry.

After the wedding, Reb Elye reminded his father-in-law—naturally in a very gentle manner—about the sum he had promised to contribute.

"Really? You actually want me to pay it? So it seems you completely deceived me."

"What do you mean, Father-in-law? I've deceived you, just because I expect the payment?"

"It's like this," smiled Reb Velvele. "You know that I'm a maggid. A maggid's way is to spice up his speech with a tasty parable, tell a tall tale, something unexpected, to draw in the audience. An intelligent listener understands that the parables and stories the maggid tells never happened at all. They're just made up. A fool thinks that the things the maggid relates really happened just as he says.

"When I promised you three hundred rubles," concluded Reb Velvele, "I took you for someone who has enough sense to understand that that was just maggid-talk. How could you imagine that I really had three hundred rubles? But now that you're insisting on the money, it seems that you're the kind of person who thinks that a maggid says the plain truth. You fooled me!"

960

A certain Jewish merchant went insane, may it never happen to us! To all appearances he was just like any of us. He spoke normally, but he suffered from particular delusions. His wife realized that he wasn't in his right mind, and she gradually took his business into her own hands until she was completely in charge, selling, purchasing, and arranging deals.

Some time passed, and the merchant's mental state still hadn't improved. His wife did everything she could to convince him to go see Reb Dovidl Tolner. But he wouldn't hear of it: he was healthy and didn't need any Rebbe's help. Still his wife kept insisting.

Once he said to his wife: "You know, you're the crazy one. You've convinced yourself of this mad idea that I'm crazy. But I'm as sane as can be."

"So you know what, then?" said his wife. "Take me to Reb Dovidl."

That made perfect sense to him, and the two of them went to see Reb Dovidl.

When they reached Tolne, they went to an inn and asked for the samovar to be heated up, as merchants with money do. After they finished their tea, he said to his wife, "I'm going to stroll around for a bit. I'll be back soon." She let him go.

He went straight to the Tolner court and spoke to Reb Dovidl. "Rebbe," he said, "I've come here with my wife. Sorry to say, she's touched in the head. She speaks like a normal person, but she's got this mad idea that I'm crazy. I'll come right back here with her, but first I wanted the Rebbe, may he be well, to be apprised of her illness."

With that, he rushed back to the inn.

A while later, husband and wife went to see Reb Dovidl.

"Holy Rebbe," wept the wife, "it's a catastrophe. My husband is touched in the head."

The husband stood off to the side, winking at Reb Dovidl and pointing at his forehead.

Reb Dovidl looked from one to the other and back, and didn't know which one was sane and which was mad.

"Give me 18 rubles as a contribution," he said to the husband.

"Give him the money," the husband told his wife.

"Aha!" said Reb Dovidl. "If she's the one responsible for the money, *you* must be the one who's sick!"

963

The great Jewish philosopher Moses Mendelssohn had a hunchback which made him very ugly. His wife was a great beauty, the daughter of a prominent and wealthy man.

How did Mendelssohn find such a match? It happened like this:

In his youth Mendelssohn was a private tutor for the children of the prominent Berlin Jew Guggenheim. He fell in love with Guggenheim's lovely, capable daughter. But she wouldn't consider him because of his hunchback.

Once, when they were sitting together chatting, Mendelssohn said to her: "Fraulein, do you believe that matches are made in heaven?"

"Yes," she answered, "I believe that."

"Let me tell you a story," said Mendelssohn. "According to the rabbis, forty days before a child is born, they announce in heaven: 'The daughter of so-and-so will be married to so-and-so.' When I heard the angel announce, 'The daughter of Guggenheim to Moses Mendelssohn,' I was very curious. I asked the angel: 'What does she look like? Is she pretty?'

"'No,' said the angel. 'She's ugly, she has a hunchback.'

"I was moved to pity my intended, and I said to the angel: 'Go to the Creator and tell him that I'd rather have the hunch on my back. Let my intended be lovely, without a flaw.'"

That won over the young woman, and she became engaged to Mendelssohn.

966

Reb Naftoli Ropshitser once visited Zakhov, a village near Melits. There were just ten adult male Jews in Zakhov, just enough for a minyan, but they had a synagogue and a cemetery.

Reb Naftoli encountered a little Jewish girl who was standing in the lane. "Tell me, child," asked Reb Naftoli. "Why do you need both a synagogue and a cemetery? Perhaps everybody will live and you'll have a minyan, so you won't need the cemetery. But if, God forbid, one of the men dies, no more minyan, you won't need a synagogue."

"The cemetery," answered the girl, "we keep for visitors."

967

Reb Elye Chaim Lodzher's intellectual gifts were already evident in his early youth. The noblemen who used to come to see his father, Reb Moyshe, enjoyed chatting with the little boy and delighting in his precocious wisdom.

When he was five, a nobleman asked him: "Tell me, where would you rather be: in Gehennom or in heaven?"

The boy responded with a question: "Who's in heaven, and who's in Gehennom?"

"Only noblemen, being Christian, get to heaven. All the Jews are in Gehennom."

"If so," responded little Elye Chaim, "I'd rather be in Gehennom with Jews than with the noblemen in heaven."

968

In the times of the Gaon, the Jewish community of Vilna was subject to a disastrous government ruling. The community sent one of its prominent leaders to the authorities in Warsaw to try to intercede.

When the man returned, he went to see the Gaon and reported that he had, thank God, gotten the ruling rescinded. He lingered for a while, looking troubled.

"What's bothering you?" the Gaon asked him.

"Rebbe," the man sighed, "I openly confess to you that in order to deal with this problem, just this once I had to break Shabbos."

"That's what's worrying you?" said the Gaon. "If you want, I'll give you a Shabbos of mine."

Shabbos and Yom Tov

511

In his youth, Reb Shmelke Nikolsburger had a friend who was deeply learned in Torah, a great prodigy who became the rabbi of Yaneve. This is a story about that friend.

One day, the rabbi of Yaneve was traveling with other relatives to a wedding. At dusk, they stopped in a forest to say the afternoon prayers. The rabbi walked off among the trees to pray by himself. The wedding guests finished their prayers and continued along their way. Because the wagons weren't going at the same pace, those in each wagon thought the rabbi must be in somebody else's carriage. And so the rabbi was left behind in the forest.

The forest was dense and vast. Night fell; it grew dark. The rabbi wandered, lost. The further he walked, the deeper he blundered into the forest. In short, he wandered like this for days and weeks, until finally he came across a human settlement and made his way home from there.

The rabbi's mind had gone a little off-kilter during his weeks of wandering, and when he got home, he was convinced that he knew which day was Shabbos and that the rest of the world was wrong. Nobody could change his mind. Thursday was Friday for him, with all the necessary preparations, ritually bathing, praying Kabboles-Shabbos, and during the day on Friday he celebrated

Shabbos in every respect.

When Reb Shmelke, who at that time was the rabbi of Shineve, heard what had happened, he traveled to Yaneve. His friend was overjoyed to see him.

"Will you stay and celebrate Shabbos with me?" he asked him.

"Yes," answered Reb Shmelke. "I came for that very reason."

Thursday afternoon, the rabbi began preparing for Shabbos—Reb Shmelke, too. They both went to the ritual bath and then donned their Shabbos garb. The rabbi welcomed Shabbos, sat down with Reb Shmelke to the Shabbos table, made Kiddush, sang zemiros—like Shabbos. Reb Shmelke, too.

At the dinner table, Reb Shmelke signaled for strong wine to be brought out. Reb Shmelke slipped one drink after another to the rabbi, who drank until he passed out, in a deep sleep. Reb Shmelke stood up, lit his pipe, and ordered that the rabbi be left undisturbed.

The rabbi slept like this the entire night and all of Friday.

Friday evening, at the Shabbos table, when Reb Shmelke had finished quietly eating, he woke up his friend. "Yanever Rabbi, get up, time for the grace after meals."

And so the rabbi was healed from his delusion.

512

Reb Boruch Mezhbuzher lived lavishly. His brother, Reb Moyshe Chaim Efroyim, the *Degel Makhne Efroyim*, was a pauper who barely got by.

Reb Boruch once came to stay with his brother for Shabbos. Reb Moyshe Chaim Efroyim ordered the finest preparations be made for Shabbos—much more than he could afford.

On Friday night, the table was covered with a pure linen cloth. On it lay a couple of small challahs, a bit of raisin wine in a small kiddush cup, and a herring with onion. Two candles burned in ceramic candlesticks. There was a homely clay vessel for the ritual washing.

They sat down at the table. Reb Boruch couldn't stop gaping at this show of great poverty.

"Why such a poor meal?" asked his brother.

"Something is missing?" asked Reb Moyshe Chaim Efroyim.

"At my home," responded Reb Boruch, "I'm used to spending Shabbos at a table decked out with only the best: silver candlesticks, a golden kiddush goblet, and a choice wine. We wash from a handsome copper vessel—everything's right and proper."

"And how do you pay for this?" asked Reb Moyshe Chaim Efroyim.

"What do you mean how?" wondered Reb Boruch. "I travel all around the world and provide Jews with spiritual guidance; naturally, they show me their gratitude."

"See," said Reb Moyshe Chaim Efroyim. "You have silver and gold at home, but you wander in exile. With me it's the opposite: the silver and gold are in exile, but I'm at home."

515

A Jew who lived in the countryside and managed an estate came to see the Belzer Rebbe, Reb Sholem Rokeach. Reb Sholem asked him where he stood in his observance of Jewish law. Did he keep Shabbos? The estate manager admitted that he couldn't observe Shabbos because the farm work couldn't wait. Reb Sholem scolded him, pointing out how holy the Shabbos is and how terrible the punishment would be for its violation. The estate manager was stricken with remorse, and said:

"Holy Rebbe, I swear to keep Shabbos all year, except harvest time, when there's too much urgent work."

"Let me tell you a story," said Reb Sholem.

> A Jew leased an estate from a nobleman. One day, the nobleman threw a big party for all of the other nobles in the area. When they were good and tipsy, they did the usual thing—they started talking about Jews. Every nobleman claimed that *his* Jew was the smartest and most loyal. The nobleman who was

hosting the party boasted, "My Jew is so faithful, you can't imagine. He'll do whatever I ask him to."

"Even convert?" someone called out.

"Yes," insisted the nobleman. "Even convert." And right away, he summoned his estate manager.

"Moshke," he asked, "are you loyal to me?"

"Yes, my lord, most certainly," answered the manager. "I'm ready to go through fire and water for my lord."

"Well then," said the nobleman, "I want you to become a Christian."

The Jew was terrified. He thought and thought, trying to find a way out, but couldn't come up with one. And he was deathly afraid of the nobleman. Finally he muttered, "Yes."

And the nobleman converted him right away.

A few months later the nobleman called for him and said, "Moshke, now you can become Jewish again."

"My lord, I will go talk it over with my wife," answered the manager.

He went home and told his wife that the nobleman had given him his permission to return to Judaism.

"Oy vey," said his wife. "What are we going to do now? Passover's just around the corner. It's so expensive: matzo, wine, dishes. Go ask the nobleman if we can stay Christian until after Passover."

522

Reb Shmuel Moliver was well-liked by all sorts of people, both observant and non-observant. Everyone respected him.

One time Reb Shmuel came to Odessa for the first congress of the Hovevei Zion. The Yiddish writer Sholem Aleichem was there as well. Sholem Aleichem proposed to a friend of his, Vassili Berman, that they go meet Reb Shmuel Moliver.

They got into a droshky and rode to the inn where Reb Shmuel was staying. They arrived at the inn, and as they got out of the droshky, they saw Reb Shmuel sitting on the balcony wearing his Shabbos clothes and studying a text. They suddenly realized that it was Shabbos. They were embarrassed, but it was too late to turn around, since Reb Shmuel had already seen them from the balcony. They climbed the stairs to his room and stood outside as if helpless.

Reb Shmuel looked at them for a while and smiled: "I see that, unfortunately, you are mortally embarrassed. Well, of course you know that in a case of life or death, saving a life overrules any Shabbos restrictions."

530

Reb Yoysef Shoyel Nathanson was extremely permissive in matters of religious law.

One time, on the day before Passover, after the time for destroying all remaining leavened food had already passed, he received a visit from Reb Moyshe Bernfeld, one of his close friends. Reb Moyshe was also sufficiently learned to rule on religious matters.

"It's a good thing you came, Reb Moyshe," said Reb Yoysef Shoyel. "People are coming here with Passover questions, but I've just been called away. Do me a favor, and stay here to answer their questions until I get back."

"Rebbe," said Reb Moyshe, "I'm not a true master of the law like you are. So if I'm in doubt, I'll rule that it's not kosher."

"Heaven forfend!" Reb Yoysef Shoyel reproached him. "If you're in doubt, rule that it's kosher. Making something kosher treyf is a worse sin than making something treyf kosher."

533

When Alexander Tsederbaum, the editor of the Tsarist-authorized Hebrew-language newspaper *Hamelits*, lived in St. Petersburg, he would always invite a few dozen guests to his Passover seders—students, writers, and doctors who were lonely for Jewish company in Christian St. Petersburg. Tsederbaum's seders refreshed their Yiddishkeit. Tsederbaum conducted a traditional seder, authentic to the smallest detail. One of the younger students would ask the four questions, Tsederbaum would explain the text of the haggadah, and everyone listened with rapt attention.

Among the seder regulars were the poet Minsky, Professor Wengroff, Ludvig Slonimsky (a son of Reb Chaim Zelig Slonimsky), and the writer S. Frug.

In Petersburg in 1881, there was a wave of conversions. A number of Jewish youth left the fold in order to receive full rights in the Russian Empire. Among them were Wengroff, Minsky, and Slonimsky.

That year Tsederbaum's seder was even livelier than usual. There were more people, including many new faces. They wanted to defiantly demonstrate their Jewishness.

While the whole crowd sat at the seder table and Tsederbaum was getting ready to make kiddush, the door opened and in walked the infamous converts—Minsky, Wengroff, and Slonimsky.

Tsederbaum stood there dumbfounded.

Suddenly Frug stood up and shouted: "Why did you stop? It's time to say, 'Pour out Thy wrath' anyway." And he began intoning, with the traditional melody, "Pour out Thy wrath upon the nations that knew Thee not.'"

Everyone began to clap, and the three converts backed away, dying from shame.

552

Tsalel Odesser, the famous cantor, led the prayers at the court of the Savraner Rebbe. He once committed a serious sin, alas! So that

Rosh Hashanah the Rebbe wouldn't let Tsalel lead the prayers. Tsalel huddled in the corner like an outcast and quietly prayed with tears running down his face while someone else led. When the cantor reached the phrase, "He who opens the gate to those who knock in repentance," Tsalel let out such a heartbroken moan that the whole congregation heard it.

The Savraner Rebbe lifted his head out from under his tallis and said, "Let Tsalel take over. He has repented."

559

Reb Yisroel, the Kozhenitser Maggid, always had a weak constitution. He was just skin and bones, barely managing to keep his soul and his body bound to one another. He wore shirts made of rabbit pelt and kept to his bed.

On Yom Kippur, he would gather all his strength to get out of bed and lead the prayers.

One year, during Kol Nidrei, when he came to the words "*salakhti kidvorekho*" (I have forgiven you as you asked), he paused for a while and began arguing with the Master of the Universe:

"Lord, no one except You knows how weak I am, and no one except You knows how strong You are. And if I could summon my last scrap of strength to go lead these prayers, all for the sake of Your children, would it be so hard for You to say for their sake just two words: *salakhti kidvorekho*?"

564

One Yom Kippur, Reb Yisroel Salanter was late to Kol Nidrei. Naturally, the entire congregation waited for him—you couldn't start until he had said Kol Nidrei. They waited and waited—it grew quite late—but Reb Yisroel still wasn't there. So the shammes was sent over to his house. No one was home! They had all gone to hear Kol Nidrei.

The congregation began to grow agitated, worrying that, God

forbid, something had happened to Reb Yisroel. So they set off in search of him. They looked and asked around, but he was no-where to be found, so they started to make their way back to the synagogue. One of them happened to glance through the window of a nearby home, and he was stunned to see Reb Yisroel sitting by a cradle and gently rocking the child inside it.

They ran into the home, crying: "Rabbi! Don't you know, we've been looking everywhere for you. We're waiting for you to do Kol Nidrei."

"Shhh," Reb Yisroel replied, "You'll wake the babe. It only just fell asleep. When I was walking to the synagogue, I heard a child's cry. So I went into this room, and no one was here. They had all gone to the synagogue. So I sat down to rock the babe, until it had fallen asleep..."

565

In the year of the plague (may we be spared), Reb Yisroel Salanter and the entire rabbinical court of Vilna announced that no one should fast that Yom Kippur, since the doctors had declared that anyone who fasted in a time of cholera would be placing himself in mortal danger.

After the morning services on Yom Kippur in the main syna-gogue of Vilna, the shammes banged his hand on the lectern and announced that everyone should go home, make kiddush, and eat the holiday feast. Nobody budged. All the men stood there wear-ing their tallis and kitl, looking at each other and then down at the ground, their eyes full of tears. You can't just pretend it's not Yom Kippur. Whose feet would obey them to go home and eat?

Reb Yisroel Salanter went up onto the platform and tried to con-vince everyone to go home and eat, arguing that the ongoing com-mandment to "guard your souls" is just as important as the one to "afflict your souls" on Yom Kippur, and that in the face of a mortal danger almost the entire Torah can be set aside. And then something happened that no one expected.

Reb Yisroel signaled to the shammes, who poured out a goblet of wine. Reb Yisroel took the goblet, pronounced a blessing in heartbroken tones, and drank the wine in front of the entire congregation.

The congregation swallowed their tears, answered "Amen," and with bowed heads slipped out of the synagogue to go home and eat for the first time on Yom Kippur.

575

Reb Yankev Kazlover was known throughout the entire region as a great scholar. Brezhan wanted to hire him as their rabbi and offered him a contract. Reb Yankev refused: he didn't want to be a communal rabbi. But his wife wanted to be a rabbi's wife, especially in a community like Brezhan. She tried to convince him to take the job, but Reb Yankev held firm.

Once, before Sukkes, his wife wouldn't leave the matter alone. She insisted he accept the position.

"You know what," said Reb Yankev, "if you buy me a really nice esrog, I'll think about it."

She immediately set off for Brezhan, and there she bought him a gorgeous esrog, not sparing a cent.

When everyone in Kozlov found out that Reb Yankev had a special esrog, they came one after the other to borrow it. And right from the first day, the esrog lost its luster. It became dark and spotty, unrecognizable as the lovely thing Reb Yankev's wife had brought home.

"You see," said Reb Yankev to his wife, "even the finest esrog loses its luster once it falls into the hands of the community."

577

Reb Chaim Sanzer had the custom of generously distributing alms before Sukkes. He would borrow from the esrog merchants and give the money to whoever needed it.

"Papa," his son once said, "giving alms is a big mitzvah. But no-where is it written that you're obligated to go into debt in order to fulfill the commandment."

"Gevalt!" shouted Reb Chaim. "How can a son be so cruel to his own father? You see your father doesn't have even a wisp of Torah, nor a scrap of piety, and now you want to take away from him this one good deed?"

578

Even as an adolescent, Reb Levi Yitschok was already known for his genius, his Torah knowledge, and his fear of Heaven. Reb Yis-roel Perets of Levertov, a wealthy and respected man, became his father-in-law and supported the young couple, as was the custom in those days. Naturally, Reb Levi Yitschok was greatly revered in Levertov: here was Torah and worldly status all wrapped up in one.

The first Simchas Torah that Reb Levi Yitschok was in town, he was offered the honor of reciting the first verse in the series be-ginning with, "You have been shown to know" (Deut. 4:35). The shammes called him up with the special flourishes for the holiday, and the whole congregation went quiet, waiting to hear the fine young man. Reb Levi Yitschok picked up his tallis, thought it over, and then put it back down. He picked it up again, then put it back down. The congregation gaped in astonishment; his father-in-law was completely mortified. Finally Reb Levi Yitschok called out, "Since you're such a scholar and Hasid, *you* go and say, 'You have been shown.'" And Reb Levi Yitschok did not go up to read.

On the way home, his father-in-law was angry. Reb Levi Yitschok was happy: it's a holiday! At the table, his father-in-law asked: "My dear Levi Yitschok, how could you embarrass me like that? What will people say?"

"My dear father-in-law, let me tell you what happened," said Reb Levi Yitschok. "When I picked up my tallis to go say 'You have been shown,' I saw the Evil Inclination there.

"'Who are you?' I asked him.

"'And who are you?' he asks me.

"I say, 'I'm a scholar.'

"He says, 'I'm a scholar too.'

"'Where did you learn the Talmud and codes?' I ask him.

"'And where did you learn?' he asks back.

"'I studied with such-and-such master,' I answer.

"'Right next to you, I was studying, too,' he says.

"'But I am a Hasid,' I say.

"'Me too,' he says.

"'Where did you study Hasidism?' I ask.

"He asks right back, 'And where did you learn it?'

"'In *Sifrey Yereim*,' I say.

"'Right by your side, I learned that, too,' he says.

"I saw that he wouldn't leave me alone, so I put down my tallis and said, 'Since you're such a scholar and Hasid, *you* go and say, 'You have been shown.'"

579

[During the Sukkes holiday, Jews beseech God for redemption while waving lulavim, in the air, and then beseech God for success while holding the lulav in place.]

Once a Jew came to Reb Yitschok Elchonon to ask whether he should emigrate to America.

"Are you making a living?" Reb Yitschok Elchonon asked him.

"Somehow I make a living," answered the Jew, "but I'm not really successful enough to be able to save even a few rubles."

"If so," said Reb Yitschok Elchonon, "you shouldn't emigrate. After all: when we ask God for redemption, we wave the lulav all around, but when we ask God for success, we stay where we are."

584

Reb Moyshe Landau, the grandson of the *Noda B'Yehuda*, lived in Uman in the time of Nikolai I. Reb Moyshe was both a Torah scholar and a Maskil. He was one of the first to become enthusiastic about the project of convincing Jews to cooperate with the government by sending their children to secular schools to make them proper bourgeois subjects.

Once, following a government decree, he gathered all the Jews into the synagogue and delivered a speech demonstrating the utter necessity of learning the national language. He pointed out that our ancestors always learned foreign languages, bringing evidence from various Biblical verses and Rabbinic statements. One of his sources was the miracle of Purim.

"Gentlemen," he said, "you all know that the miracle of Purim started with Mordecai saving Ahasuerus' life. Mordecai informed the king that his two courtiers, Bigsan and Teresh, were plotting to poison him. How did Mordecai find out about this? He overheard a conversation between the two courtiers. What were they speaking? Persian, the state language. Now just imagine, gentlemen,"—here his voice rose, and his hands flew in the air—"imagine if Mordecai was like today's rabbis, and he didn't know the national language. He wouldn't have understood the courtiers' conversation, Ahasuerus would have been poisoned, and Haman could have done to the Jews whatever his wicked heart wanted."

"An error in exegesis, Mr. Modernizer!" called out a Hasid. "On the contrary, that story just goes to show that Jews usually did *not* learn 'Goyish.' If they had, the courtiers would have been more careful when speaking in front of Mordecai."

586

One Purim in Lemberg, a member of the congregation who was both wealthy and learned sat studying in the study house. The rabbi, Reb Yoysef Shoyel, saw this and was furious. He walked over, closed the man's book, and ordered him to leave the study house.

"Your place on Purim is not here in front of the Talmud. Go home to your pile of coins and hand them out to the paupers."

973

Reb Akiva Eiger was once told that a certain Jew had ridden the train on Shabbos.

"Really?" said Reb Akiva. "It's not enough that he breaks Shabbos, but he has to be a thief, too?"

"A thief?" everyone wondered. "Who did he rob?"

"The government," smiled Reb Akiva. "He didn't buy a ticket for the two angels that keep him company on Shabbos."

975

Reb Zalmen Poyzner, the rabbi of Warsaw, didn't think much of the Hasidim's exaggerated piety. He couldn't stand people who made strange faces and wriggled their bodies while they prayed.

When he lived in the country on his estate at Kuchar, a Hasid once came to spend Shabbos with him. Before Shabbos, the Hasid asked in a quavering, over-pious tone: "Will you be able to get fish for Shabbos here in the country?"

"And if there's no fish?" teased Reb Zalmen, putting on a straight face.

"Ay," sighed the Hasid, "according to the Hasidic books, there is a great mystical secret to eating fish on Shabbos."

"Don't vex yourself," said Reb Zalmen. "God willing, there will be fish for Shabbos."

Friday night, Reb Zalmen sat down at the table with the members of his household and all his guests. Everyone got a generous portion of fish. The Hasid, however, got a whole small fish. He wondered why he was being treated worse than everyone else. But he didn't say a word out of respect for the host. At lunch, it was the same thing. Everyone got a big portion of fish, but the Hasid got a tiny whole fish. The Hasid ate, utterly despondent, feeling smaller than everyone else.

When the time came to prepare for the third meal of Shabbos, the Hasid couldn't contain himself. He asked Reb Zalmen, "Please tell me, why didn't I get the same portion of fish as everybody else last night and at lunch?"

"Well," answered Reb Zalmen, "everybody was given fish to eat. But you wanted fish just for the secret it contains. Now, who knows exactly which part of the fish might contain the secret? So they gave you a whole fish, to make sure you got the secret."

990

Nisn Rozental was famous throughout the Jewish communities of Lithuania as someone who ridiculed traditional Judaism. It made his day to play a prank on a pious Jew, trip him up and somehow make him sin.

Nisn was a wealthy man, an important contractor who built highways for the government. Wherever one of his new highways stretched, the surrounding towns prospered, since Nisn was by nature generous and open-hearted.

One Tisha B'Av afternoon, while Nisn was supervising the construction of the highway from Vilna to Minsk, he rode to a small town in the Vilna region. When he arrived in his fine carriage, he went straight to the rabbi's house. He went in and said: "Rebbe, I've come to ask you whether I might be permitted to eat something even though it's a fast day. I'm feeling—may it not happen to you—very weak, and it's hard for me to fast."

The rabbi looked at this healthy Jew with his ruddy face and fat neck and said: "No, I can't permit you to eat. What do you think, Tisha B'Av doesn't matter? It's almost as strict as Yom Kippur."

"I know, Rebbe," Nisn responded, putting on a pious air. "But I really feel like I'm not going to make it if I don't eat. By the way, I'll make up for it with a big donation to atone for not fasting. Since your town doesn't have a bathhouse, I'll order my workmen to build you a fine one."

The rabbi, a simple-minded man, heard these words, looked at Nisn again and asked him: "So you're saying, you really can't make it through the fast?"

"Can't make it?" Nisn heaved a sigh with great apparent vexation. "I feel like I'm going to pass out. Already my vision is going!... And I'll build you a bathhouse, Rabbi, that will make the whole region jealous."

The rabbi thought it over for a while, and murmured to himself: "A matter of life and death...who am I to judge, as the Talmud says, 'the heart knows its own bitterness'..." He turned to Nisn and said: "Well, in that case, you can eat something."

"Please tell me, Rabbi," asked Nisn, "where can I find something to eat? After all, nobody in town's going to give me anything to eat on Tisha B'Av. Go try telling one of them that I have a weak constitution and the rabbi said I could eat. Rabbi, maybe it would make sense for you to send one of your servants to pick up something I could eat here?"

"Sure, I'll do that," said the rabbi.

Nisn provided money, and a servant soon came back from the marketplace with several bagels, a herring, and a bottle of liquor. Nisn washed, made a blessing, and sat down at the table.

Suddenly he got up, hurried over to the rabbi and cried: "Oy, Rabbi, look how you look, like a dead corpse, God forbid!"

The rabbi, who was an elderly gentleman and worn out from fasting, became quite frightened.

"Rabbi," Nisn insisted, "you must not fast a minute longer. And if you don't eat, I won't either, and both our souls will be on your account."

The rabbi began to waver. "Well, I am feeling rather weak."

Nisn wouldn't let it go. "Rabbi, you go wash *right away*. You know what, I'll offer a second donation to make up for your breaking the fast. I'll send one of my people to build a fence around the town cemetery."

The rabbi was convinced. He washed, made a blessing, and sat down next to Nisn at the table.

Nisn poured him shot after shot. The rabbi's eyes got squintier and squintier, his face grew redder and redder, and his yarmulke slipped to the side of his head.

"You know, Rabbi," Nisn remarked, "Moshiach was of course born on Tisha B'Av. And I tell you—that's the best reason of all to dance!" Saying which, he threw his arm around the rabbi's shoulder, and began to circle the table, clapping his hands and singing the Purim song, "The rose of Jacob exulted and rejoiced."

And so it drew on toward evening. Everyone was waiting in the study hall for the rabbi to come so they could daven minchah. Nobody would start minchah on Tisha B'Av without the rabbi. After all, you wait all day to put on your tallis and tefillin, and there are all of the special prayers... They waited and waited, until they couldn't wait any longer. They sent the shammes to summon him. The shammes entered the rabbi's house and couldn't believe his eyes: The rabbi could barely stand up straight, and he was singing and dancing as if it were Simchas Torah.

The town was in an uproar. It's unheard of! A drunken rabbi on Tisha B'Av! It never happens anywhere in the world.

Nisn Rozental vanished immediately.

After Tisha B'Av, the community board called a meeting and fired the rabbi.

When Reb Hillel Amtshislover, who was at that time the rabbi of Krakow, heard about this incident, he immediately went to the town and ordered the rabbi reinstated.

He said to the heads of the community: "Your rabbi really did something stupid. But you were even more stupid to retain for decades a fool like that as your rabbi. You've put up with him this long, you can put up with him a while longer."

Index of Names

Note: Mordekhai Lipson here provided, in addition to the names of individuals as they appear in the stories, additional names by which they were known, such as the titles of their best-known works or a surname. Each entry, however, refers to only one individual.

The index lists the page, with the story number in parentheees.

About the Author

Mordekhai Lipson was born Mordechai Yavorovsky in Bialystok in 1885. He attended the Radiner Yeshiva as a teenager before becoming a collector, writer, and Yiddish and Hebrew translator of secular and religious folklore in the States and Israel. He died in Tel Aviv in 1958.

About the Translators

Jonathan Boyarin is the Diann G. and Thomas A. Mann Professor of Modern Jewish Studies at Cornell University. His most recent previous book is *Yeshiva Days: Learning on the Lower East Side* (Princeton).

Jonah S. Boyarin is a writer, educator, and Yiddish translator. His original work and translation has been published in *In Geveb*, *Ayin Press*, and *Jewish Currents*. He is currently a doctoral student at Columbia University.

Recent books from *Ben Yehuda Press*

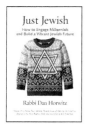

Just Jewish: How to Engage Millennials and Build a Vibrant Jewish Future by Rabbi Dan Horwitz. Drawing on his experience launching The Well, an inclusive Jewish community for young adults in Metro Detroit, Rabbi Horwitz shares proven techniques ready to be adopted by the Jewish world's myriad organizations, touching on everything from branding to fundraising to programmatic approaches to relationship development, and more. "This book will shape the conversation as to how we think about the Jewish future." —Rabbi Elliot Cosgrove, editor, *Jewish Theology in Our Time*..

Judaism Disrupted: A Spiritual Manifesto for the 21st Century by Rabbi Michael Strassfeld. "I can't remember the last time I felt pulled to underline a book constantly as I was reading it, but *Judaism Disrupted* is exactly that intellectual, spiritual and personal adventure. You will find yourself nodding, wrestling, and hoping to hold on to so many of its ideas and challenges. Rabbi Strassfeld reframes a Torah that demands breakage, reimagination, and ownership." —Abigail Pogrebin, author, *My Jewish Year: 18 Holidays, One Wondering Jew*

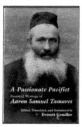

A Passionate Pacifist: Essential Writings of Aaron Samuel Tamares. Translated and edited by Rabbi Everett Gendler. Rabbi Aaron Samuel Tamares (1869-1931) addresses the timeless issues of ethics, morality, communal morale, and Judaism in relation to the world at large in these essays and sermons, written in Hebrew between 1904 and 1931. "For those who seek a Torah of compassion and pacifism, a Judaism not tied to 19th century political nationalism, and a vision of Jewish spirituality outside of political thinking this book will be essential." —Rabbi Dr. Alan Brill, author, *Thinking God: The Mysticism of Rabbi Zadok of Lublin*.

Seeking the Hiding God: A Personal Theological Essay by Arnold Eisen. "This generation's preeminent scholar of contemporary Jewry, Arnold Eisen has devoted his career to studying the spiritual strivings within the Jewish soul. In *Seeking the Hiding God*, Eisen provides a personal window into his own theological vision. Eisen's explorations will inspire readers to ask today's urgent questions of meaning and faith." —Rabbi Dr. Elliot Cosgrove, author of *For Such a Time as This: On Being Jewish Today*.

Embracing Auschwitz: Forging a Vibrant, Life-Affirming Judaism that Takes the Holocaust Seriously by Rabbi Joshua Hammerman.The Judaism of Sinai and the Judaism of Auschwitz are merging, resulting in new visions of Judaism that are only

beginning to take shape. "Should be read by every Jew who cares about Judaism." —Rabbi Dr. Irving "Yitz" Greenberg

Put Your Money Where Your Soul Is: Jewish Wisdom to Transform Your Investments for Good by Rabbi Jacob Siegel. "An intellectual delight. It offers a cornucopia of good ideas, institutions, and advisers. These can ease the transition for institutions and individuals from pure profit nature investing to deploying one's capital to repair the world, lift up the poor, and aid the needy and vulnerable. The sources alone—ranging from the Bible, Talmud, and codes to contemporary economics and sophisticated financial reporting—are worth the price of admission." —Rabbi Irving "Yitz" Greenberg.

The Way of Torah and the Path of Dharma: Intersections between Judaism and the Religions of India by Rabbi Daniel Polish. "A whirlwind religious tourist visit to the diversity of Indian religions: Sikh, Jain, Buddhist, and Hindu, led by an experienced congregational rabbi with much experience in interfaith and in teaching world religions." —Rabbi Alan Brill, author of *Rabbi on the Ganges: A Jewish Hindu-Encounter*.

Recent books from *Ben Yehuda Press*

Burning Psalms: Confronting Adonai after Auschwitz by Menachem Rosensaft. "It's amazing that Menachem Z. Rosensaft's *Burning Psalms: Confronting Adonai after Auschwitz* doesn't burst into flames. This book of poetry — every poem in it a response or counterpoint to every one of the psalms in the biblical book — written by the son of Holocaust survivors and the brother of a murdered sibling he never knew, is composed with fire, fueled by a combination of rage, love, and despite-it-all faith that sears your eyes as you read it." —*New Jersey Jewish Standard*

Weaving Prayer: An Analytical and Spiritual Commentary on the Jewish Prayer Book by Rabbi Jeffrey Hoffman. "This engaging and erudite volume transforms the prayer experience. Not only is it of considerable intellectual interest to learn the history of prayers—how, when, and why they were composed—but this new knowledge will significantly help a person pray with intention (*kavanah*). I plan to keep this volume right next to my siddur." —Rabbi Judith Hauptman, author of *Rereading the Rabbis: A Woman's Voice.*

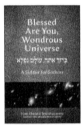

Blessed Are You, Wondrous Universe: A Siddur for Seekers. Non-theistic Jewish prayers by Herbert J. Levine. "Herb Levine has fashioned a sparkling collection of prayers for a thinking, feeling modern person who wants to express gratitude for the wonder of existence." —Daniel Matt, author, *The Essential Kabbalah*. "An exercise in holy audacity." —Dr. Shaul Magid, author, *The Necessity of Exile*

Siddur HaKohanot: A Hebrew Priestess Prayerbook by Jill Hammer and Taya Shere. Creative and traditional Jewish rituals and prayers that explore an earth-honoring, feminine-honoring spirituality with deep roots in Jewish tradition. "Far more than a prayerbook, this is a paradigm-shifting guidebook that radically expands our religious language, empowering us to reclaim what our souls have known for centuries: how to cook, season, and feast on our love of life, Spirit, and each other." —Rabbi Tirzah Firestone, author, *The Receiving: Reclaiming Jewish Women's Wisdom*

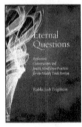

Eternal Questions by Rabbi Josh Feigelson. These essays on the weekly Torah portion guide readers on a journey that weaves together Torah, Talmud, Hasidic masters, and a diverse array of writers, poets, musicians, and thinkers. Each essay includes questions for reflection and suggestions for practices to help turn study into more mindful, intentional living. "This is the wisdom that we always need—but maybe particularly now, more than ever, during these turbulent times." —Rabbi Danya Ruttenberg, author, *On Repentance and Repair.*

Musar in Recovery: A Jewish Spiritual Path to Serenity & Joy by Hannah L. with Rabbi Harvey Winokur. "A process of recovery that is physically healing, morally redemptive, and spiritually transformative." —Rabbi Rami Shapiro, author of *Recovery: The Twelve Steps as Spiritual Practice*. "A lucid and practical guidebook to recovery." —Dr. Alan Morinis, author, *Everyday Holiness: The Jewish Spiritual Path of Mussar.*

Other Covenants: Alternate Histories of the Jewish People by Rabbi Andrea D. Lobel & Mark Shainblum. In *Other Covenants*, you'll meet Israeli astronauts trying to save a doomed space shuttle, a Jewish community's faith challenged by the unstoppable return of their own undead, a Jewish science fiction writer in a world of Zeppelins and magic, an adult Anne Frank, an entire genre of Jewish martial arts movies, a Nazi dystopia where Judaism refuses to die, and many more. Nominated for two Sidewise Awards for Alternate History.